Targeting
Iran

I Targeting ran

DAVID BARSAMIAN

with NOAM CHOMSKY,
ERVAND ABRAHAMIAN,
and NAHID MOZAFFARI

Open Media Series
City Lights Books
San Francisco

The Open Media Series is edited by Greg Ruggiero and archived by
the Tamiment Library, New York University.

Cover photo by Ali Khaligh. "An Iranian couple cross the street in downtown
Tehran, Iran, 2005."

Cover design: Pollen

Library of Congress Cataloging-in-Publication Data
    Barsamian, David.
    Targeting Iran / by David Barsamian; with Noam Chomsky, Ervand Abra-
    hamian, and Nahid Mozaffari.
    p. cm. — (Open media series)
    Includes index.
    ISBN-13: 978-0-87286-458-0
    ISBN-10: 0-87286-458-8
    1. United States—Foreign relations—Iran. 2. Iran—Foreign relations—
    United States. 3. United States—Foreign relations—1945-1989. 4. United
    States—Foreign relations—1989- 5. Iran—Politics and government—
    1941-1979. 6. Iran—Politics and government—1979-1997. 7. Iran—Politics
    and government—1997- I. Chomsky, Noam. II. Abrahamian, Ervand, 1940-
    III. Mozaffari, Nahid. IV. Title.
    E183.8.I55B38 2007
    327.7305509'045—dc22
  2006101938

City Lights Books are published at the City Lights Bookstore,
261 Columbus Avenue, San Francisco, CA 94133.

Visit our Web site: www.citylights.com

ERVAND ABRAHAMIAN, born in Iran, is professor of Middle Eastern history at Baruch College in New York. A leading scholar on Iran, he is the author of *Iran Between Two Revolutions* and *Khomeinism*, and coauthor of *Inventing the Axis of Evil*.

DAVID BARSAMIAN is the award-winning founder and director of Alternative Radio (www.alternativeradio.org). His interviews appear in magazines and periodicals around the world. His latest books are *Speaking of Empire and Resistance* with Tariq Ali; *Imperial Ambitions* with Noam Chomsky; and *Original Zinn* with Howard Zinn.

NOAM CHOMSKY, internationally renowned MIT professor, practically invented modern linguistics. In addition to his pioneering work in that field, he has been a leading voice for peace and social justice. The *New York Times* calls him "a global phenomenon, perhaps the most widely read voice on foreign policy on the planet." A prolific author, his latest books are *Failed States* and *Interventions*.

NAHID MOZAFFARI, born in Iran, is author of *The Public Intellectual in Iran: 1906–1956*. She has taught Middle Eastern history at the New School in New York. She received her Ph.D. in history and Middle Eastern studies from Harvard.

■ ▪ ▫

Contents

ACKNOWLEDGMENTS

I would like to thank all the contributors who made this book possible. Additionally, my gratitude goes to Anatascia Dadashpour for her astute editing assistance, Farah Davari for her sagacious advice, David Peterson, fact-checker extraordinaire, KGNU for technical support, and Greg Ruggiero, intrepid editor. Thanks also to *International Socialist Review,* where parts of the Chomsky interview appeared.

—David Barsamian

■   ■   ■

Introduction

BY DAVID BARSAMIAN

"Iran encompasses some of the most critical geography in the world, [which] gives it a critical position from which adversaries could interfere with oil flows from the Arab states that border the Persian Gulf. Apart from geography, Iran's oil deposits are important to the long-term health of the world economy."
—RONALD REAGAN, November 13, 1986

"The actions and policies of the Government of Iran continue to pose an unusual and extraordinary threat to the national security, foreign policy, and economy of the United States."
—GEORGE W. BUSH, executive order extending the national emergency with respect to Iran, March 10, 2005

"There are very few countries on the face of the earth that have caused us more trouble than Iran, more heartburn than Iran over a period of decades."
—LEE HAMILTON, Iraq Study Group, PBS's *The NewsHour with Jim Lehrer*, December 2006

"Iran," area specialist Dilip Hiro writes, "is unique in geography, history, and culture. Its shoreline runs along the eastern side of the oil-rich Persian Gulf and about 300 miles (480 km) of the Arabian Sea. It is a neighbor of the six Arab Gulf monarchies. It has land borders with the Indian subcontinent, Afghanistan, Turkmenistan, Azerbaijan, Armenia, Turkey, and Iraq; and it shares its Caspian Sea littoral with Russia and Kazakhstan."

Iranian identity is deeply rooted in its millennia-old civilization. In the ancient world, the Persian Empire dominated much of what is now called the Middle East. Iranians are proud people and aware of their history and culture.

Iran is a multilingual, multiethnic country. Farsi, an Indo-European language, is the national language. It is written in the Arabic script from right to left. Its grammar, however, is completely different from that of Arabic, which is a Semitic language. The Iranians added four letters to the twenty-eight of the Arabic alphabet to accommodate some singular Persian sounds. Farsi, probably originating in the Fars area of central Iran, is a powerfully expressive and beautiful language with a great tradition of poetry. The most well-known of its poets is Rumi, the mystical Sufi. Rumi's work has been translated into many languages, and today he is one of the most widely read poets in the world. When I was in

Iran, I heard Rumi couplets recited by shopkeepers and students. In addition to "Maulana" Rumi, the list of Iran's great classical poets includes such giants as Hafez, Sadi, Attar, Jami, Khayyám, and Nizami. The tradition of poetry and its importance in Iranian culture continues today, as Nahid Mozaffari discusses in chapter 4. The country's national epic is *The Shahnameh,* by Ferdowsi. Iran also has its own very rich classical music system based on modes, or *dastgah.*

Although an ancient land, Iran today is a youthful country. Approximately one-third of its 70 million people are under thirty years of age. Women are probably better educated than in any other country in the region. They make up 65 percent of all students entering university. In addition to their strong presence in education, medicine, and the arts, many women are anchors, reporters, and talk-show hosts on TV and radio programs. However, their representation in top government positions is not as prominent.

Ethnically, Iran is composed primarily of Persians, but there are significant Azeri, Kurd, and Arab minorities. Although an Islamic republic, Iran contains small communities of Baha'is, Armenian

Christians, Jews, and Zoroastrians. Zoroastrianism, a monotheistic faith, was founded by Zarathustra in 1200 BC. It was the major religion in Iran until the Arab conquest of the seventh century. Under the Arabs, Iran became Muslim.

Shah Ismail of the great Safavid Dynasty established Shia Islam as the state religion in 1501. Today, 89 percent of Iranians are Shia, more than in any other country. Because of its massive Shia population, Iran's historical, cultural, and religious links with neighboring Iraq are deep. The principal pilgrimage sites for Shias worldwide, not just Iran, are the shrines in Najaf (Imam Ali) and Karbala (Imam Hussein) in Iraq.

In the modern period, Iran has been the center of great power rivalries. First czarist Russia, then the Soviet Union, competed with Britain for supremacy in Iranian affairs. Since the end of World War II, the United States has projected its military, diplomatic, and economic power on Iran and the Middle East. For good reason: Iran has huge oil and natural gas reserves. The area constitutes, in the words of a 1945 State Department document, "a stupendous source of strategic power, and one of the greatest material prizes in world history" (Chomsky and Barsamian, *Imperial Ambitions*, 2005, p. 6).

In late October 2006, the United States deployed a "strike group" of military vessels to the Persian Gulf, including a nuclear aircraft carrier, a cruiser, a destroyer, a frigate, a submarine escort, and a supply ship, as well as Marine Corps units, just off Iran's coast. The task force was dubbed the Eisenhower Strike Group. The former president's name has special resonance for Iranians. It was Eisenhower who approved the 1953 coup overthrowing the democratically elected government of Mohammed Mossadegh. The latter, a popular figure, had the temerity to believe that Iran's oil wealth should benefit the Iranian people. Clearly, Mossadegh did not understand the basic rule of international relations as explained by top State Department planner George Kennan: it is "our oil." So when Mossadegh nationalized the oil wells, Washington, egged on by London, overthrew him. The shah was restored to power. His tyrannical rule set the stage for the rise of Ayatollah Ruholla Khomeini. *Ayatollah*—"sign of God"—is the supreme Shiite clerical title.

The 1953 coup is one of the central events of

twentieth-century history, and its repercussions continue to this day. Yet most Americans know little about Iran and the coup against Mossadegh. Ask the average American about the hostage crisis, however, and I am certain you would get a much higher level of recognition. Mark Bowden's *Guests of the Ayatollah* (2006), for example, is a 680-page book with only four references to Mossadegh. Bowden's book received extensive media coverage and hit best-seller lists. One cannot understand the November 1979 takeover of the U.S. embassy in Tehran and the hostage crisis, the subject of his book, without the context and background of the 1953 coup. The coup, code-named "Ajax," was directed by Kermit Roosevelt and run out of the U.S. embassy in Tehran. Twenty-six year later, the militants, with some reason, feared a rerun. Months before the seizure of the embassy, President Jimmy Carter dispatched Robert Huyser, a top general, to Tehran to inspire a countercoup using sympathetic elements in the Iranian military. Huyser did not succeed.

The 1953 coup was doubly significant; it not only terminated the democratic experiment and brought back the shah, but it effectively ended British influence in Iran. The United States was now in the driver's seat, exactly where it wanted to be. Marginalizing the British and also the French in the region was one of Washington's primary policy goals in the post–World War II era. So the Iranian coup was a big step in realizing their geopolitical objectives. For Iranians, the events of 1953 are not ancient history. Their memories of the destruction of their democracy are vivid. And the memories extend beyond Iran. While I was on a lecture tour of Lebanon and Syria in 2005, whenever I mentioned the coup, members in the audience were well informed about its details and ramifications.

Under the shah, Iran was a cornerstone of U.S. hegemony in the Middle East for more than twenty years. Iran and Israel were, as Nixon's defense secretary Melvin Laird said, local "cops on the beat" ensuring that "radical nationalists" would not threaten U.S. interests.

The Islamic Revolution of 1978–79 ended that equation and altered regional power dynamics. With the overthrow of the shah, Iran severed itself from the United States. Not only did the United States lose one of its main regional allies, but the new government in Tehran signaled the end to the flow of Iranian cash going to U.S. military contractors. The shah had spent tens of billions of dollars purchasing U.S.-made weapons. He had also, with Washington's blessing, embarked on a nuclear energy program.

Today, the United States and Iran are on the brink of war. Much of what we see playing out today had its origins in the events of the late 1970s. The "loss" of Iran was a huge blow to Washington's larger strategy in the Middle East. The humiliating and interminable hostage crisis, coupled with a botched rescue mission, further hardened Washington's stance toward the new government in Tehran. The United States cut off diplomatic relations and imposed sanctions, conditions that continue to this day.

The Reagan administration's diplomatic, military, and economic support for Saddam Hussein's 1980–88 war on Iran deeply embittered Tehran and strained relations even further. However, Washington was playing both sides. In the mid-1980s, it was covertly selling arms to Iran in a complicated scheme to fund the Contras in Nicaragua. Tehran went along with this deal because most of its military arsenal was of American origin and it was desperate for spare parts. Once the details became public, and the Iran-Contra scandal embarrassed and weakened the Reagan presidency, shipments ceased.

Under George W. Bush, U.S.–Iranian relations have deteriorated drastically. In his 2002 State of the Union address, President Bush designated Iran as part of the "axis of evil." The speech stunned Tehran, particularly as it had just assisted the Bush administration in ousting the Taliban in Afghanistan. The "axis of evil" label was a big setback for reform president Mohammad Khatami (1997–2005), who risked much in cooperating with the United States. For Iran to be categorically grouped with Saddam Hussein's Iraq, which had waged an eight-year war against Iran (1980–88), was an additional humiliation.

In March 2003, the United States invaded Iraq. That May, Khatami sent a broad-range proposal to Washington through the Swiss embassy. According to a March 2007 article by Craig Unger in *Vanity Fair*, the Iranian offer was "comprehensive" and "everything was on the table—Iran's nuclear program, policy toward Israel, support of Hamas and Hezbollah, and control over al-Qaeda operatives captured" by Iran. "Given the initiative's historic scope, however," Unger writes, "it was surprising when the Bush administration simply declined to respond. There was not even an interagency meeting to discuss it." A few days later, the White House had the State Department reprimand the Swiss ambassador "for exceeding his diplomatic mandate" in conveying the Iranian proposal, writes Unger, citing National Security Council staffer Flynt Leverett. For Tehran not to receive a reply from Washington was yet another insult. During my February 2007 trip to Iran, a hard-liner told me, "We told Khatami not to deal with the Americans. We told him, you will get nothing for your efforts. He didn't listen to us."

Political tensions with the United States have sharply escalated in 2006–7. United States allies Israel, India, and Pakistan all possess nuclear weapons but have not signed the Nuclear Non-Proliferation Treaty (NPT). Washington gives those countries a free pass, but not Iran, which is a signatory to the NPT and has come under intense scrutiny. As a signatory to the treaty, it is permitted to enrich uranium. However, it is accused by the Bush administration, with some European support, of enriching uranium to develop nuclear weapons.

The International Atomic Energy Agency, based in Vienna, referred the issue of Iranian compliance or noncompliance with the NPT to the UN Security Council in New York. In December 2006, the Security Council voted to impose limited sanctions on Iraq. More comprehensive sanctions, with the United States pressing the issue, are on their way. Interestingly, the United States is also a signatory to the NPT and, as such, is obliged to draw down its nuclear weapons arsenal. Despite their importance for understanding the crisis, it is virtually impossible to find mention of these key facts in most U.S. media reporting on the issue.

The central tenet of U.S. policy is: What we say goes. To make certain Tehran understands this basic principle of statecraft, in February 2007 Washington has dispatched yet another aircraft carrier battle group to the Persian Gulf to join the already deployed Eisenhower group. The new armada is led by the carrier USS *John C. Stennis.*

One can only imagine the response from Washington if Iranian naval vessels were deployed offshore from New York or Seattle.

The U.S. position on talking with Iran is: Give us what a negotiation would produce before the negotiations start. You concede, and then we can sit down and talk. This posture is a nonstarter as far as the Iranians are concerned. On February 27, 2007, Iran's foreign minister, Manouchehr Mottaki, restated his country's position: "Demands that Iran halt enrichment are illegal and illegitimate." That will "never" happen, he said. However, he added, Iran is prepared to negotiate about its nuclear program "without any preconditions."

With no sense of irony, Washington constantly accuses Iran of "meddling" in the affairs of its neighbor Iraq. In January 2007, Bush warned that American military forces would "seek out and destroy" Iranian "networks" in Iraq. Washington accuses Iran of supplying Iraqi insurgents with explosively formed projectiles (EFPs). These EFP accusations threaten to spark a conflict with Iran in the same way that the issue of weapons of mass destruction was used by United States to justify its war on Iraq. Although the Bush administration says it has no intention to invade Iran, the *New Statesman* and the BBC, on February 19 and 20, 2007, revealed detailed plans of what an American attack would look like. The BBC reported that two triggers would cause U.S. military action: (a) any confirmation that Iran was developing a nuclear weapon or (b) if Iran were responsible for a high-casualty attack against U.S. forces.

As Iraq slides further into sectarian chaos, movement is occurring across the region. A "shift is occurring," write Michael Slackman and Hassan Fattah in the *New York Times* on February 6, 2007, "with encouragement from the Bush administration. Its goal is to see an American-backed alliance of Sunni Arab states including Saudi Arabia, Jordan, Lebanon and Egypt, along with a Fatah-led Palestine and Israel, opposing Iran, Syria and the radical groups they support." The article goes on to say, "While the Bush administration sees the conflict in Iraq as one between allies and terrorists, the Saudis tend to see it as Sunnis versus Shiites—and they favor the Sunnis, while the Americans back the Shiite-led government."

If U.S. strategy in the Middle East is fueling the Shia–Sunni divide, the prospects for a regional war become more probable. Seymour Hersh, in his March 5, 2007, *New Yorker* article titled "The Redirection," says, "The 'redirection,' as some in the White House call the new strategy, has brought the United States closer to an open confrontation with

Iran and, in parts of the region, propelled it into a widening sectarian conflict between Shiite and Sunni Muslims." Hersh continues, "To undermine Iran, which is predominantly Shiite, the Bush Administration has decided, in effect, to reconfigure its priorities in the Middle East." Hersh goes on to say that one aspect of Washington's new policy is "the bolstering of Sunni extremist groups that espouse a militant vision of Islam and are hostile to America and sympathetic to Al Qaeda." Hersh reports that the United States is carrying out "clandestine operations aimed at Iran," including putting special forces inside that country. The United States, in another aspect of its Iran destabilization strategy, is attempting to stir up discontent among various ethnic groups, such as the Azeris, Kurds, Arabs, and Baluchis. Saudi money and influence, according to Hersh, are a crucial factor in the "redirection."

Once again, as in the Iran-Contra and the Afghan mujahideen episodes, Washington turns to Riyadh, one of the most extremist regimes on Earth, for aid and support. Saudi Arabia is positioning itself as the defender of the Sunnis not just in Iraq but also in Lebanon. This strategy, in coordination with

Washington, can have explosive consequences, not just in the region but in south Asia, where there are Shiite minorities. The sectarian war in Iraq could be just the beginning of much greater bloodshed. And that is because of the intolerant Wahhabi Islam practiced in Saudi Arabia.

Wahhabism was founded by Mohammed Abdul Wahhab in the eighteenth century. Its central tenet is a literal interpretation of the Koran. Its antipathy and hostility to Shia Islam, the predominant Islam practiced in Iran, Iraq, Bahrain, and Azerbaijan, are profound and unyielding. Scholar Vali Nasr gives some background: "The rise of Islamic fundamentalism in South Asia and the Arab World in the 1970s on lent new intensity to age-old anti-Shia bias." This trend was bankrolled largely by Saudi money. In the Saudi's Wahhabi worldview, Shia Islam is seen as apostasy. "Wahhabis," Nasr continues, "condemned the [Shiite] veneration of saints and their shrines as polytheism, and viewed Muslims who engaged in this action as heretics. . . . [I]n 1802 Wahhabi armies invaded Karbala and desecrated the shrine of Imam Hussein—an event that has left an indelible mark on Shia historical memory." Nasr adds, "As Wahhabism has become increasingly influential across the Muslim world and become the theological driving force behind Salafist movements [such as al-Qaeda], the tenor of the Shia–Sunni conflict has become more strident. In many ways the greater violence of Shia–Sunni conflict in recent years flows from the spread of Wahhabi influence." Washington is playing with fire in relying on Wahhabi fundamentalists in Saudi Arabia. That President Bush and Secretary of State Condoleezza Rice could both describe the regime in Riyadh as "moderate" is staggering.

The Bush administration's anti-Iranian propaganda has had an effect on U.S. public opinion, which now, according to Gallup, regards Iran "most negatively of 22 countries" and as America's "greatest enemy." In addition to the usual suspects beating the drums of war against Iran, such as the *Weekly Standard*, the American Enterprise Institute, and CNN's Glenn Beck, radical Christian fundamentalists are joining the fray. Televangelist John Hagee warns, "Iran is the command post for global Islamic terror." Author Jerome Corsi writes, "A world ruled by Iran is something every person who loves freedom should fear."

On the domestic political front, I think the

Democrats will try to outflank the Republicans, by staking out an even more aggressive position on Iran. United States security will continue to be wedded to Israel's, and anyone who doesn't have the stomach for military action against Iran will be branded an appeaser. Few will risk the stigma of being labeled soft on Iran. Whenever the discussion turns to Iran, leading presidential candidate Hillary Clinton repeats the war hawks' mantra, "All options are on the table."

Shirin Ebadi, Iran's 2003 Nobel Peace Prize laureate, in an opinion piece in *USA Today*, has this advice for Americans and the regime in Washington: "The Iranian people are exceedingly proud of their 2,500-year history and culture. Iran as a country is larger and greater than its rulers and exists apart from any government in power at any particular time. If America attacks, however, Iranians will unite, forgetting their differences with their government, and they will fiercely and tenaciously defend their country."

Her comments were made real to me during my 2007 trip to Iran. In conversations I had with many Iranians, even those opposed to the government, they all told me that war talk and any U.S. military action would be counterproductive. It would generate further support for President Mahmoud Ahmadinejad and the clerics. Washington's belligerent rhetoric, they told me, has made it extremely difficult for what are called moderate reformers to express themselves, thus further consolidating power for the religious hard-liners. Those criticizing the government are portrayed as being tools of the Americans.

I met with Shirin Ebadi in May 2006 when she was visiting Denver to give a lecture. She told me, "Democracy cannot be brought to a people with cluster bombs. Any military invasion, or even the threat of one, harms democracy. It is not something that happens overnight. Democracy needs to evolve in a peaceful atmosphere. And the U.S. should not impose it on Iran or any other country. It will be a disaster if it tries."

I asked Ebadi if she liked Iranian poetry. She smiled and replied, "There is hardly an Iranian who does not have an appreciation for poetry. I read poetry at night. It helps me relax."

I asked her to recite a couplet she particularly liked. She picked one from Hafez that says,

If there is no justice,
then those who are deprived
    may one day take to the streets and rise up.

The purpose of this book is to offer a primer on the escalating crisis between the United States and Iran, to provide the reader with critical background information often omitted when U.S. media discuss Iran, and to introduce readers to some of the deeper political and cultural issues at play in contemporary Iran. The interviews presented here were all conducted at various times throughout 2006.

Targeting Iran

NOAM CHOMSKY

Bush administration rhetoric on Iran reflects similar comments it made about Iraq. The president calls Iran "the world's primary state sponsor of terrorism"; the secretary of state calls Iran's record "something to be loathed"; Defense Secretary Rumsfeld said "the Iranian regime is today the world's leading state sponsor of terrorism." And accompanying that rhetoric is the media echo chamber. A recent Newsweek *cover story titled "The Next Nuclear Threat: How Dangerous Is Iran?" used a grim photo of the Iranian president, Mahmoud Ahmadinejad. Where is U.S. policy going on Iran?*

U.S. policy has been fairly consistent with regard to Iran for over half a century. There are variations depending on circumstances, but the guiding principles are the same. Here people sort of pretend it's ancient history. The people who hold the clubs typically like to forget history and say it's irrelevant. But the people who are hit by the clubs tend to remember history, for good reasons, because it teaches you something. They are correct in this. If we want to learn about it, we should stand alongside the victims.

Crucial, relevant parts of U.S. policy toward Iran begin, of course, with the overthrow of the parliamentary government in 1953 by a U.S.[-led], British-backed [and] initiated military coup, which installed the shah—one of the more brutal tyrants of the last half century—and supported him fully to the end. A couple of months before he was overthrown, President Carter was telling him how much the Iranian people love him because he's so marvelous, and so on.

He was overthrown in 1979. There were American hostages taken at the time of the crisis. The only event that exists in American history is that hostages were taken, not twenty-five years of terror and torture after the overthrow of the parliamentary government. But Iranians look at it differently. This is their history. Ever since that time (1979), the U.S. has tried to destroy the government. Right away Carter sent a NATO general to try to instigate a military coup, but it didn't work.

The U.S. had close relations with the Iranian military. They started providing the Iranian military with arms—that's the way you overthrow a civilian government: you arm the military, via Israel, with Saudi Arabian money, which makes sense because Iran, Saudi Arabia, Israel, and Turkey were the regional allies in controlling Middle East oil. That didn't work. With various twists and turns, it eventuated in the Iran-Contra affair. Meanwhile the U.S. supported Iraq's war against Iran. Iraq invaded Iran in September 1980.

Saddam Hussein was executed for crimes that he committed in 1982. If we had a properly functioning free press in the country, it would have pointed out that 1982 is quite an important year in U.S.–Iraqi–Iranian relations. That was the year in which Reagan took Iraq off the list of states supporting terror. And the reason was so that he could provide Iraq with aid, including means to develop weapons of mass destruction, nuclear weapons, biotoxins, chemical weapons, and so on. At that time it was primarily for the war against Iran, although the same aid continued long after that war was over. There were other reasons. Donald Rumsfeld, whom you quoted, was sent to Iraq to finalize the deal with their friend Saddam. The Iranians don't forget this. They lost a huge number of casualties to the U.S.-backed Iraqi aggression. They were attacked with chemical weapons and other atrocities.

The punishment of Iranians continues until today. The basic reason is simply that Iran disobeyed orders. Overthrowing a U.S.-installed tyrant is not acceptable behavior, and in one or another way the Iranian people have to be punished for it. So they've been under harsh sanctions, now threats of attack—not just threats, preparations for attack.

Israel is a small country, but it's now more or less a U.S. offshore military base and high-tech center. Thanks to the U.S. connection, it has a very powerful military. Its air force is larger and technologically more advanced than any NATO power outside the United States. For the last couple of years the United States has been sending over one hundred advanced jet bombers to Israel, very publicly advertised as capable of, with the intention of, bombing Iran. These jets are equipped with what are called "special weapons" in the Hebrew press. No one knows what that means, but it's for the ears of Iranian intelligence. They're supposed to make a worst-case analysis.

The invasions of Iraq and Afghanistan surround Iran with U.S. forces, in the Gulf and Central Asia as well. Pakistan has nuclear weapons, but the major nuclear power in the region is Israel. It has hundreds of nuclear weapons and presumably other weapons of mass destruction. Iran is simply surrounded by hostile forces.

The invasion of Iraq was a very clear signal, quite well understood everywhere, that if you want to deter a U.S. invasion, you have to have some kind of deterrent. One deterrent is terror. Another deterrent is nuclear weapons. So the invasion of Iraq was basically a plea to Iran to develop nuclear weapons. And that's understood. One of Israel's leading military historians, Martin van Creveld, wrote in the *International Herald Tribune* that of course Israel doesn't want Iran to get nuclear weapons, but if they're not doing it, they're "crazy," given the strategic situation and the U.S. invasion of Iraq.

Let's come closer to the present. Three years ago, the European Union and Iran made a bargain. Iran says they're enriching uranium for the development of nuclear energy. If that's what they're doing, it's entirely within the framework of the Nuclear Non-Proliferation Treaty (NPT). In fact, it's little bit ironic at MIT, where we are now, I should say, because twenty years ago MIT made a deal with the shah of Iran, pretty much to sell him a large part of the nuclear engineering department. The deal was that MIT would train lots of Iranian nuclear engineers and in return the shah would pay some big sum of money. That leak led to a huge protest on campus by students who were overwhelmingly opposed to it. The faculty overwhelmingly approved it. All of this was done, if not at U.S. government initiative, certainly with its support. At that time Henry Kissinger was explaining that Iran needs nuclear energy. It has to preserve its petrochemicals for other purposes. Now Henry Kissinger—he's just a symbol, the same with everyone—is saying they can't possibly need nuclear energy, they have so much petroleum reserves, so they must be developing nuclear weapons. Kissinger was asked about this, and he said [that] they were an ally then, so then they needed nuclear energy; now they [have broken] out of U.S. control, so they don't need nuclear energy. Enrichment of uranium, which is legal under the NPT, is not a long step from developing nuclear weapons. So who knows? Maybe Martin van Creveld is correct and they're not crazy. I don't know.

Anyway, three years ago the European Union did make a bargain with them that Iran would stop enriching uranium, though they're legally entitled to do it, and in return—here's the other half of the bargain—the European Union would provide firm guarantees on security issues. The phrase *security issues* refers to U.S.–Israeli threats to bomb Iran, which are very serious.

By U.S. standards, Iran ought to be carrying out terrorist acts in the United States. In fact, adopting U.S. standards, we ought to be demanding that they do it. They're under far greater threat than anything Bush or Blair ever conjured up, and that's supposed to authorize what they call *anticipatory self-defense*, namely attack. They can't bomb the United States. They could do something else. Of course, that's totally outrageous, but that just tells you something about U.S.–British standards. However, Europe did not live up to its half of the bargain. Apparently under U.S. pressure, it backed off. It did not make any offer to provide any guarantees of security. Shortly after, Iran backed off from its side of the bargain.

That brings us up to the present, with Europe refusing to live up to the bargain; the U.S. and Israel continuing, extending in fact, the threats to Iranian security, which are serious; and Iran, we don't know. They're back to enriching uranium, and we don't know for what purposes. No one wants Iran to get nuclear weapons. If there were a real interest in preventing that, what would happen is you would reduce the threats, which are making it likely that they'll develop them as a deterrent; implement the bargain that was made; and then move toward integrating Iran into the general international economic system; remove the sanctions, which are against the people, not the government; and just bring them into the world system. The U.S. refuses. Europe does what the U.S. orders them to do.

One of the problems that the U.S. is facing is that China is not intimidated. That's why the U.S. is so frightened of China. You see headlines on the front pages, "How Dangerous Is China?" Of all the major nuclear powers, China has been the most restrained in its development of offensive weaponry. But China is frightening because it is not intimidated. Europe will back off, and China won't. European companies, frightened of the U.S., have backed away from investments in Iran, but China just proceeds. That's why the U.S. is so terrified of China.

If you're the Mafia don and somebody doesn't pay protection money, that's scary, especially when you can't do anything about it.

What may happen is that the Bush administration may succeed in driving Iran into the Asian energy security system. Iran has options. They might decide that Europe is much too cowardly to stand up to the U.S. and decide that they'll break their ties with the West and turn eastward. There is an Asian energy security grid linked to the Shanghai Cooperation Organization [SCO]. It's based in China and Russia. The Central Asian states have joined. India will probably join—it's unclear. India and Iran are observers at the SCO. South Korea will probably join. Iran wants to develop an independent energy security system for this rapidly growing industrial region in Asia. That's a very frightening prospect for the United States, because it reduces U.S. global domination. If Iran joins the Asians, it could be a kind of lynchpin. Iran has plenty of natural gas, substantial petroleum, and so on. And the U.S. may drive them into that grid, which would strengthen it. And that's expanding.

China, as I say, is not intimidated. They're also making deals with Saudi Arabia, which is the main center of energy production. I forgot the exact number, but I think they're getting maybe 10–15 percent of their energy imports from Saudi Arabia. They're also entering into military relations both with Iran and Saudi Arabia. With Iran, it's presumably because the two countries regard it as a deterrent to U.S. threats. With Saudi Arabia, it's extremely frightening to U.S. planners. The U.S. military catastrophe in Iraq, which is one of the worst in history, may end up leaving Iraq with a Shiite majority, with pretty close relations with Shiite Iran. A lot of the clerics, including the Ayatollah Sistani, come from Iran. The major militia in the south, the Badr brigade, was trained in Iran and actually fought with Iran during the Iran–Iraq war.

These ties have already been increasing. Moqtada Sadr leads the Mahdi army, the other major militia. By attacking him, the U.S. has turned him from a minor cleric into a major figure in Iraq. He gained, I think, 50 percent or so in the last parliamentary elections and is now on a par with the other major Shiite bloc. He may end up being the leading element in the Shiite bloc. He was in Tehran recently and announced that if the U.S. or Israel attacks Iran, his militia—and the U.S. is afraid maybe the

Moqtada Sadr

Iranian army—will join in attacking the U.S. in Iraq. That could blow up. We don't know. The Pentagon doesn't know. Nobody knows. That's one of the deterrents. And it could end up being the ultimate nightmare for Washington: a Shiite bloc, including Iran, Iraq to the extent it attains any sovereignty, and the Shiite areas of Saudi Arabia, which are adjacent to the other two countries, and which happen to be where most of Saudi Arabian oil is. That conceivably could be an independent, loose Shiite alliance controlling most of the world's oil, not subordinated to the U.S., possibly even joining the Asian energy security grid. If the Bush administration achieves that, they will have seriously undermined the U.S. position in the world.

Moving elsewhere, they're doing the same thing in the Western Hemisphere. Their talent for alienating allies is phenomenal. They've even succeeded in alienating Canada, and that takes tremendous talent. But the Bush administration has refused to follow NAFTA judgments in favor of Canada in Canada–U.S. cases. The U.S. just told them to get lost after they ruled against the United States. Canada is not very happy about it. They don't stand up to the U.S., but they didn't like it. And the gov-

Seller of U.S. crude

ernment has said that if this continues, they'll divert oil that they're sending to the U.S. to China. Canada is one of the major energy providers to the United States.

The other major provider in the Western Hemisphere is Venezuela. U.S. hostility to Venezuela has also driven them to diversify. They have increasing relations with China. And they are quite happy to do it. They're diversifying their exports. And from Venezuela down to Argentina, the region is almost out of control. The U.S. doesn't have the mechanisms it used to have, like military coups and attacks and so on. It can't do that anymore. In fact, they tried. In 2002, they did try to support a military coup in Venezuela to overthrow the government. That's the standard technique. But they had to back off very quickly. Run

There was a huge uproar in Latin America, where democracy is taken more seriously than in Washington, which had to back away and turn to subversion. They are also losing the economic controls. The main economic stranglehold for Latin America has been basically the offshoots of the Treasury Department: the IMF [International Monetary Fund], and the World Bank. They have led

Latin America into economic disaster almost everywhere, and they're now being kicked out.

Argentina, which was the poster child for the IMF, had a terrible economic collapse following IMF rules. They managed to recover, but only by radically violating the rules. They are now, as Néstor Kirchner, [Argentina's] president, says, ridding themselves of the IMF, paying off the debt, with no more contact with the IMF. They're being helped by Venezuela, which bought up part of their debt. Bolivia will probably do the same. It's been the same IMF–World Bank catastrophe for the last twenty-five years. And if the U.S. loses its economic stranglehold over Latin America and can no longer carry out military attacks—which is not so obvious, incidentally; the U.S. is considerably increasing its military forces there—if those economic controls are gone, it almost certainly won't have anything like the degree of control it's had before. That includes major resource producers, oil in particular. Venezuela and Canada aren't going to drift very far. But even if they do a little, if you add that to what they might do in the Middle East, it's going to change world affairs considerably.

If the Asian energy security grid expands and

Nestor Kirchner

43

if—an even worse nightmare for Washington—it includes Iran as a sort of a lynchpin, possibly even Shiite Iraq and Saudi Arabia, they're sooner or later likely to diversify their financial reserves. They're held in dollars. That's part of what's propping up the U.S. economy. These countries have enormous financial reserves, along with Japan, the biggest in the world. If they diversify to other currencies, which is probably going to come sooner or later, that's going to be a major blow to the international financial system. Nobody knows what would happen, but it would be significant. And, yes, the threats against Iran, which are very serious and criminal, in fact—

Why do you say that?

Take a look at the UN Charter. The threat of force is ruled out—the threat *or* use of force. But the threat alone is ruled out. We accept that, for example, if somebody threatened us. It is official U.S. and British policy that if there is any threat of force against the U.S. and Britain—threat, not act—they can carry out anticipatory self-defense. They can attack the country. That's what happened in Iraq. In

44

fact, France just went along with that. President Chirac said a couple of weeks ago that if any country threatens France with weapons of mass destruction, France is free to attack it. In fact, what he said is any country that is considering the use of weapons of mass destruction is subject to attack by France. Commentators were polite enough not to point out that what he was saying is that the French air force ought to be dropping nuclear bombs on Paris, because, as he announced, France is considering the use of weapons of mass destruction and therefore should be a target of attack by French nuclear forces. Put aside his little logical lapse. But that's an expansion, a corollary to the British–U.S. position.

And, yes, it's the typical imperial mentality. No one can consider the use of force against us, certainly not threaten, obviously, not prepare for it. That would be outlandish. But we can do it against them. In fact, that's considered very righteous. The people at the other end of the club don't necessarily see it that way.

A report in late January 2006 in the Los Angeles Times, *titled "57% Back a Hit on Iran if Defiance Persists," shows that support for military action against*

Iran has increased over the last year even though public sentiment is running against the war in Iraq. Is that a paradox?

No, it's not a paradox. In fact, there are figures and polls that look like paradoxes. So, for example, take Iraq. I've forgotten the exact numbers, but a fairly large percentage, maybe two-thirds of the population, thinks it would have been wrong to invade Iraq if it had no weapons of mass destruction; and even if it had an intention to do so, it would have been wrong to invade. On the other hand, about half thought it was right to invade Iraq even though the fact that they had no weapons of mass destruction had been officially conceded long before and the public knows it. That looks like a direct contradiction. But Steven Kull, the director of the institute that runs the polls—the Program on International Policy Attitudes which is the major one—pointed out that it's not really a contradiction. People still believe that Iraq had weapons of mass destruction, even though it's been officially conceded that they don't.

What does that mean? He didn't go into it, but what it means is that the government–media propaganda campaign was extremely effective in instilling fear. People think they're defending themselves. Even if it's already been conceded that the threat was not there, and maybe concocted, the fear still remains. And it's the same with Iran. If you read enough of those articles you cited, you will think we're in mortal danger if Iran gets a nuclear weapon. What danger are we in, even if Iran does get a nuclear weapon? They're not going to use it except as a deterrent. If there were even an indication that they were planning to use it, the country would be vaporized. So it's there for a deterrent. But people can be frightened by massive propaganda. It's not a surprise.

Take a classic example, Germany. Under the Weimar Republic, Germany was the most civilized country in the world, the leader in the sciences and the arts. Within two or three years it had been turned into a country of raving maniacs by extensive propaganda—which, incidentally, was explicitly borrowed from Anglo-American commercial propaganda. And it worked. It frightened Germans. They thought they were defending themselves against the Jews, against the Bolsheviks. And you know what happened next. It can be done. And it was done to an extent in the U.S., as well, by very effective propaganda.

You're seeing it again today. So, for example, just do a media search and find out how often it has even been mentioned that when Iran began enriching uranium again, it was after the Europeans had rejected their side of the bargain, namely, to provide firm guarantees on security issues. That means no guarantees that Iran will not be attacked, which is no trivial matter. Of course, when one partner to a bargain backs down, we expect the other to back down in reaction. Ask if that has been mentioned once in the media in the U.S. anywhere. It's not that the press doesn't know it. Of course they know it. At least, if they read the international business press they know it. For example, in mid-January [2006] there was a very good article about it by Selig Harrison in the *Financial Times*, the leading business paper of the world. You think they didn't read it at the *New York Times* news desk or editorial board? Sure they read it. But that's not the kind of thing you report. I don't have the facilities to do a search, but I'd be willing to bet that that's not even been mentioned in the mainstream in the United States.

Or that Iran is virtually surrounded by U.S. military forces in Afghanistan, Iraq, Turkey, and the Persian Gulf.

If that were mentioned, which it may be, it's because we're defending ourselves, just like Hitler was defending himself against the Jews.

Has anyone ever done research on the real cost of oil to the U.S. when you factor in Pentagon spending, the ground troops, the naval and air bases in the Middle East, and the stockpiles of WMDs [weapons of mass destruction] and conventional weapons?

I know of only one attempt to do it. It was by Alfred Cavallo, an energy consultant. He did a study—I don't want to quote the figures from memory, but it was something like, if you count in the military, it amounts to a subsidy of 30 percent of the market price of oil. But it's not the full story. Military spending and bases may be costly to the American taxpayer, but policy is not designed for the benefit of the population, it's designed for the benefit of power sectors. And for them it's useful to dominate the world, by force if necessary. And also don't forget that Pentagon spending, though it's a cost to the taxpayer, is profit for the corporations. It depends what you think the country is. If you think the country is its population, yes, it's a big cost. If you think the country is the people who own the country, no, it's a gain.

I should say, the same is true of other things, like a lot of concern about the enormous U.S. trade deficit. How we are going to deal with it? Economists tear their hair out. It's a catastrophe. If you assume that the U.S. consists of its people, yes, there is a huge trade deficit. On the other hand, if you assume that the U.S. consists of the people who own the country, which is more reasonable, the trade deficit goes way down. Then, for example, if Dell is exporting computers from China to the United States, it would be considered U.S. exports, not U.S. imports. And it is from the point of view of the Dell management. Then the trade deficit shoots way down. You can read about that in the *Wall Street Journal*. It's not a big secret. The business world understands it. And they don't say it, of course, but they act, and the *New York Times* acts, and the government acts, as if the country is the people who own it. And that's not surprising. They're among the people who own it, so why shouldn't they look at it that way? Simply ask yourself how many pages are there in the press devoted to business affairs and how many are devoted to labor? Most of the people in the country are labor, not owners of stock. The ownership of stock is very highly concentrated: the top 1 percent owns maybe half of it, and most people own essentially nothing. The stock market and business affairs are huge issues. But labor affairs doesn't even have a reporter covering it. That expresses the same comprehension of what the country is.

Tariq Ali suggests that unchallenged U.S. military power could lead to more aggression and war in order to mask its economic weakness.

It's possible. A predator—some lion on the march— can be dangerous, but a wounded one is much more dangerous. Then it may act in ways which are unpredictable. The same is true in international affairs. The Bush administration has turned the U.S. into a monstrous attack instrument, but a wounded one. And that's a very threatening state of affairs. In fact, the Bush administration is quite consciously increasing the threat of nuclear terror against the United States. It's increasing the threat of general terrorism in many, many ways. And it's conscious. Not because they want it, but because it just doesn't matter that much, it's a low priority.

Take the invasion of Iraq. It was perfectly well understood, and they learned from their own intelligence agencies and others, that the attack was likely to increase proliferation of weapons of mass destruction for deterrence and to increase terror. And so it did. In fact, it did so in unanticipated ways. It was expected that it would probably increase terror, as in fact it did, but what about weapons of mass destruction? You read that it was discovered by the official U.S. investigations, the Duelfer and Kay reports, that Iraq didn't have the means to develop weapons of mass destruction. That's not exactly correct. It did. They were there: the ones that were provided to Saddam Hussein by Britain, the U.S., and others, as long as he was obeying orders. They were being dismantled but they were still there, under guard by UN inspectors.

The UN inspectors were kicked out. Rumsfeld, Cheney, and the rest didn't think it was interesting to tell their troops to guard the sites, so they were systematically looted. The inspectors continued their work by satellite, and they reported that over one hundred sites had been systematically looted, meaning not just somebody goes in and steals something, but carefully looted. And they described the equipment that was in them. It was high-precision machine tools and others that could be used to develop missiles and nuclear weapons, lethal biotoxins that could be used for biological weapons. All that went somewhere. That's expanding the threat of weapons of mass destruction. We all hate to guess where it went, but you can make a guess. That's well beyond the threat to the United States that was anticipated from the invasion of Iraq.

I met a Jordanian journalist, who was part of a Swedish journalists' program, who informed me that he was at the Jordanian–Iraqi border through this period. He said the border guards were reporting that one out of every eight trucks that was coming from Iraq into Jordan under the U.S. occupation was testing positive for radioactive materials. There is a name for this; in fact, Rumsfeld had a nice phrase for it: *Stuff happens.* Stuff happens, and it's not that they're trying to increase the threat to the United States. It's just that it doesn't matter that much.

That can bewilder some people, because these are intelligent, smart people, educated at the best universities. Why would they pursue a policy that seems to threaten their interests?

Depends what you think their priorities are. They have two fundamental interests. You have to be willfully blind not to see it. The basic policies of the administration are not obscure. To put it as simply as possible, policy one is to stuff the pockets of your rich friends with as many dollars as possible. Policy two is to get into a position where you can shake your fist at the world so that people will do what you want them to do: intimidate the world by force. The invasion of Iraq achieved those aims. Nobody at Halliburton is complaining that they're going broke. In fact, the same companies that provided Iraq with the weapons are now being paid to do what they call "reconstruct Iraq," which means to rob the U.S. taxpayer blind. The amount of corruption and robbery under the occupation has just been colossal. So they're making out fine.

I think everyone assumed that the invasion would be a walkover. Iraq was completely defenseless. They knew it. They had already been bombing it for a year. We know that now, even if we did not before.

"Spikes of activity."

Which they kept secret, because Blair and Bush and the guys around them hate democracy so much that they know you must not allow the population to know what you're doing. But they were doing it. And we now know about it, some of it at least. And Iraq was defenseless. They should have been able to walk in. It should have been one of the easiest military occupations in history, but they managed to turn it into a catastrophe. It looked as though they would easily be able to control Iraq, which means gaining control of the second-largest hydrocarbon reserves in the world and significantly increasing their domination of Middle East oil production. That would provide the U.S., as Zbigniew Brzezinski put it, with "critical leverage" over its major rivals, Europe and the Asian industrial systems.

Those are policies that go back to right after the Second World War. As George Kennan said, we may not need Middle East oil or even want it, but controlling it gives the U.S. "veto power" over others. If you have your hand on the spigot, you can determine what they will do. We just saw an illustration of this when Russia turned off the spigot to the Ukraine, and Europe was facing an energy crisis. Nobody expects the U.S. to do that, but just the poised fist is a very good instrument of control. So it's a rational policy.

If it happens to be threatening to the American population, it's not a priority. That's not who they're working for. When they cut taxes for the rich, is that for the benefit of the population? Read this morning's headlines. If they concealed the fact that the levees had broken in New Orleans for two days, is that in order to help the population? It's just not a priority.

The new Bush budget includes big increases in spending on the military and domestic security and cuts in social programs.

It just follows from the two simple principles: enrich your rich friends as much as possible, increase your power over the world, and somebody else will take care of the rest. If you have to cut Medicaid for the poor, well, who cares about them? There are almost 40 million people going hungry, who don't have money to buy food. Does that matter? They're not influential, so who cares what happens to them?

The owners of the economy and the managers of the state have children, grandchildren. Certainly in the areas you're describing, of increasing military threats, they're putting their own lives and the lives of their families in peril. Again, it doesn't seem logical.

Here you have to distinguish between people in their human existence and their institutional role. A corporate executive or an official in the Pentagon may be the nicest guy in the world, takes care of his children, plays with them, cares about them. But in an institutional role he may act in such a way as to endanger their lives. After all, they have legal obligations. For corporate executives, their legal obligation is to maximize profit and market share. They're not allowed to do anything else. It would, in fact, be a violation of corporate law. That's their legal obligation, part of the institutional role. And that goes across the board.

Just go back to the case I mentioned that took place right here at MIT back in the 1970s, about providing Iran with the means to develop nuclear energy. The students were overwhelmingly opposed. There was a referendum. The faculty approved it by about the same margin. The faculty are just the students of a couple years ago. So what happened in between? Did they get smarter or something? No. They shifted their institutional role. When you're a student, you're relatively free. That's the freest time of your life. You're out of parental control, more or less; you don't have to worry about providing for a family. You're free to think and act. When you're a faculty member, you're part of the institution. You support institutional priorities. And the same people who were students a couple years before took exactly the opposite position from the students after they had shifted the institutional role. That's very common. It doesn't mean that their personalities have changed. It has nothing to do with that.

That's why you find euphoria in business circles over the election of a president whose policies grossly oppose their own values. CEOs tend to have what are called liberal values: they don't have any objection to gay rights, they want abortion rights, so on and so forth. On the so-called cultural issues, they're kind of like college faculty. On the other hand, if you read the business press the day after the [November 2004] election, there was euphoria in boardrooms. Why? Because this government is going to give a free run to business. And if it turns out that that destroys the lives of our grandchildren, well, it's not our institutional role to worry about that. As a person I may, but not when my task is to maximize power and profit.

In early February 2006, the thirty-five-nation Board of Governors of the UN's International Atomic Energy Agency voted to refer Iran to the UN Security Council over its nuclear program. There is a possibility of sanctions being imposed on Iran.

There is not only a possibility. The U.S. has had sanctions on Iran ever since they disobeyed orders.

Right, but in terms of UN-imposed sanctions à la Iraq.

They were called UN sanctions on Iraq, but that's just propaganda. They were U.S. sanctions administered through the UN because the UN is afraid to stand up to the U.S. But everybody who has paid attention knows there is virtually no support for those sanctions outside of the U.S. and Britain. They're called *UN sanctions* because then it sounds as if somebody else is doing it. They were U.S. sanctions which were devastating the society. And if the UN, under the U.S. fist, passes some kind of sanctions [against Iran], which, frankly, I think is questionable, they will be U.S. sanctions again.

Do you know anybody else in the world aside from the U.S. and Britain who is in favor of the sanctions? The Europeans aren't. They want to invest in Iran. They had to pull out—they didn't have to, but they did. Many corporations ended investment. And they explained why. You can read it in the *Wall Street Journal*. They said, in effect, "We just don't want to offend the U.S. It's too dangerous." International affairs is very much like the Mafia. You don't offend the don. It's dangerous. Especially if the don is wounded. You never know what he's going to do.

But Iran has a weapon to fight back with in terms of putting the choke on its oil supply, and that would have a deleterious effect on the global economy. It's the fourth-largest producer of oil in the world.

I'm not sitting in meetings of Pentagon planners, but I think the hawks would like that, because that would give them an excuse to bomb Iran. It might even give them an excuse to invade. If you look at the geography, Iranian oil is concentrated in the Gulf area, which happens to be substantially Arab Shiite. I'm no military expert, but I presume it's within the military capacity of the U.S. to occupy that area as well as to keep the shipping lanes open. And if Iran tried to close them, and they might very well try to do that, who knows what it would lead to? Maybe we would blow Iran up and the world would blow up. But it's not a high priority. Any more than they care that they are compelling Russia and China to sharply increase their offensive military forces aimed at the U.S., to put their missiles on hair-trigger alert, which strategic analysts just call an accident waiting to happen. Not leftists, incidentally. Former senator Sam Nunn, a serious and respectable conservative who has been in the lead in efforts to cut back on the threat of nuclear war, warned recently that we may be developing an Armageddon of our own making. Maybe, but if you're a White House planner, that doesn't matter much. So, yes, if Iran did try to choke off the Strait of Hormuz, Pentagon planners might take that as an excuse to prove that we not only have to bomb Iran and kill its people, but also occupy its oil-producing areas.

Something similar happened during the Iran–Iraq war. U.S. support for Iraq was so strong that the U.S. essentially patrolled the Gulf in Iraqi interests. And just in order to make sure that Iran understood it, a U.S. naval vessel shot down an Iranian airliner, apparently in Iranian commercial airspace, killing 290 people. George Bush I was then president and seems to have thought that was fine. He said something about how he would never apologize for U.S. military actions. Iranians might not have liked it, and may even remember it without too much pleasure.

Not content with their success in Iraq, neocon stalwart Bill Kristol in the Weekly Standard *(July 24, 2006), writes, "We might consider countering this act of Iranian aggression"—that's what he calls the Lebanon war—"with a military strike against Iranian nuclear facilities. Why wait? Does anyone think a nuclear Iran can be contained? That the current regime will negotiate in good faith? It would be easier to act sooner rather than later. Yes, there would be repercussions—and they would be healthy ones, showing a strong America that has rejected further appeasement."*

As Kristol certainly knows, the shoe is on the other foot. The Iranian government has been proposing negotiations for years. We now know, and he undoubtedly knows, that in 2003 the Khatami government, the moderate government, but with the approval of the hard-line clerical rulers, offered to negotiate all outstanding issues with the United States. That included nuclear issues. It also included a two-state settlement for the Israel–Palestine problem, which Iran officially supports. The Bush administration didn't reject the negotiation offer. It didn't even reply to it. Its response was to censure the Swiss diplomat who brought the offer.

It continues. It's the U.S. that's refusing negotiations. The big hoopla now is about how Condi Rice has shifted policy, that now they're willing to negotiate seriously. That's not true. They're willing to negotiate if Iran concedes the result of the negotiations before the negotiations. So the negotiations are conditional on Iran stopping uranium enrichment, which it's legally entitled to do, which is supposed to be the goal of negotiations. So, yes, we'll negotiate if they first concede in advance. And also with a gun pointed at their heads, because we won't withdraw the threats. They made it very clear. We continue the threats, which are a violation of the UN Charter, of course, and they have to agree in advance to what we want them to do, and then we'll negotiate along with Europe. So, in other words, the U.S. is still refusing to negotiate seriously.

Iran's government is not a nice government, to put it mildly. There are all kinds of hideous things you can say about it. But the fact is, on this issue, they're the ones who offered negotiations. They're the ones who said that they would accept the two-state settlement on Israel–Palestine, the international consensus that we reject. In fact, it goes beyond that. The issue of enriching uranium to weapons grade is a very serious problem. The fate of the species depends on it. If that continues, we're not going to survive much longer. There are proposals as to how to deal with it. The major one comes from Mohamed ElBaradei, the head of the International Atomic Energy Agency [IAEA] and 2005 Nobel Prize laureate, and highly respected. His proposal, a couple of years ago, was that production of weapons-grade fissile materials be under international control and supervision, and anyone who wants to apply for fissile materials can apply to the IAEA for peaceful use. That's a very sensible proposal. As far as I'm aware, there is only one country in the world that's accepted it—Iran. Try to find a reference to that somewhere. But they did officially, through Ali Larijani, their main negotiator. It's known. So, again, plenty of criticisms. Iran has a horrible and repressive government, undoubtedly. But in these domains its position is more forthcoming than that of the United States. Do they mean what they say? That we don't know, but we do know how to find out: explore the possibility. Refusal to do that suggests concern that they might mean it seriously.

What are the prospects of a U.S. military attack on Iran?

As for a strike against Iran, you can read the analyses by people like Sam Gardiner, who runs war games for the Pentagon. He's very muted, he can't say things strongly, but it doesn't take much to understand that he thinks it would be totally insane, that the consequences could be utterly unpredictable. What the U.S. or Israel would probably do, most military analysts believe, is not go after the nuclear sites. For one thing, they don't know where they are and they might miss them. They would probably just do carpet bombing to try to destroy as much as of the country as possible, except the region near the Gulf. That's the area that they want to preserve and maybe occupy.

I have no idea what's going on inside the government, nor does anyone. Governments retain secrets from their main enemies, and their main enemy is the domestic population. If you look at the record of declassified documents, what you find is, yes, there is a concern for security, primarily security of the state against its domestic enemy. They don't want people to know what they're up to. And now they're not telling us what they're up to. But if I were sitting in a Pentagon strategy office and given the ludicrous mission of developing a strategy, I know what I think I would do: try to support a secessionist movement in the Arab area and then say, "Okay, we're going to defend the secessionist movement from the dictatorial government, and we'll bomb the rest of the country to smithereens. We'll use

Henry Kissinger's orders. You have to go back to the Nazi archives to find anything similar. When Nixon told Kissinger that he wanted to bomb Cambodia, Kissinger's orders to the military were, "Anything that flies or anything that moves" in rural Cambodia. In other words, genocide. He remains an honored figure. It was particularly interesting to watch the nonreaction to that when it was published in the *New York Times*. And I presume that would be the approach to the rest of Iran, if they can hold on to the oil-producing areas.

What this could lead to is just indescribable. They would blow up everything in Iran; they could blow up the whole region. One thing it would almost certainly lead to is what the Lebanon war is probably going to lead to: new generations of *jihadis*—bitter, angry, committed to revenge, hating those who did this to the country. It's now conceded openly that, yes, that was the effect of the Iraq war. In fact, it was anticipated that that would be the effect. Okay, it's now conceded. It went well beyond what was expected. I don't think that's necessarily going to affect the planners, because they don't care very much about terror. The domestic population is not a high concern of theirs. There are other concerns that are much higher. And if it leads to large-scale terror, "stuff happens." So it's conceivable that they might do it. I can't imagine that they would simply launch an attack, but provocations and naval deployments could easily lead to that.

2

The Mullahs Face Off:
Washington Versus Tehran

ERVAND ABRAHAMIAN

Compare the crisis with Iran to Iraq.

If you've been following U.S.–Iran relations, it's almost a rerun of the war with Iraq, with a similar cast of characters, similar images of mushroom clouds, similar language about Hitler, the axis of evil, and pitfalls of appeasement.

In one significant way, however, there is a difference. In the year 2000, a group of neoconservatives who were determined to have war with Iraq came to power in Washington. They then planned, schemed, plotted, hyped up dangers, even forged documents, and eventually got what they wanted, which was war. One has to hand it to them, they were one hundred percent successful. You can say the operation was successful. The patient may have died, the patient being more than 3,000 Americans and probably 150,000 Iraqis, but basically the neo-conservatives got what they wanted, which was an invasion and destruction of the Iraqi state.

With Iran, the situation is very different. The neoconservatives are no longer in the driver's seat. However, as much as those who are still around might want to get rid of the Islamic Republic, I think they are rational and sensible enough to realize that they're not in a position to invade and occupy the country. So they're not even thinking about a replay of Iraq. And this is quite openly stated. The neocon group that's called the Committee on the Present Danger—this was the group that masterminded the attack on Iraq—more or less disbanded after the invasion. But in the June of 2004, they came to life again with a paper on Iran. They openly stated that they weren't out to really invade Iran. They didn't say why, but reading between the lines you know why. They've given up the policy of military confrontation and occupation. They actually talked of things such as negotiations, diplomacy, the opening of an embassy, and all sorts of things which they had earlier denounced people like Powell for wanting. So there was a change in policy from the neoconservative side.

Iran is a focal point of attention for the Bush administration. It is one of the original members of the "axis of evil." The war drums seem to be beating in ways that are rhetorically similar to those that preceded the attack on Iraq. Is Iran next?

I would say the present crisis is not so much of a group wanting war and planning it and therefore getting it. The danger is actually something else. The danger is a war coming from miscalculation, misjudgment, and misperceptions.

It's worth keeping in mind that most wars in the modern age from 1870 to 2001 were only wars from miscalculation, misconception, misjudgment, the two exceptions probably being the Franco-Prussian War of 1870 and the Iraqi War. One could even make a case that World War II was due to misjudgment rather than planning for the type of war that was obtained. In the present situation, what we're seeing on both sides, both in Washington and Tehran, is a gross misjudgment, misperception, miscalculation. And, of course, neither side, when push comes to shove, is willing to back down. So the danger is that both sides will escalate the crisis and before you know it things could get out of hand.

Both sides are playing brinkmanship, raising the stakes, expecting the other side to blink, chicken out, and consequently building themselves into a situation where it would be a major loss of face, which both the Occidentals and the Orientals are very concerned about, and then actually triggering off a crisis that would escalate into a major war here.

It would be incremental movements toward war rather than plans for war. The U.S. will go to the UN and try and get a sanctions resolution, expecting that if they acted tough the Iranians would back down. But the Iranians would see this in the tradition of imperial ultimatums, which they're used to. And in Iranian history, politicians who have given in to ultimatums are usually seen as traitors. The ones who have stood up against ultimatums are seen as national heroes.

In this particular case of nuclear energy, it's seen as a crucial birthright of Iran to have a full nuclear cycle. What does that mean? I think the regime intentionally leaves it vague. A "full cycle" does not necessarily mean industrial mass production. It could mean high grade for experimental and scientific purposes without mass production for weapon use. If Washington was interested, it could pursue this issue and limit Iran to limited production for civilian use. I suspect ElBaradei thinks along those lines. I can't see Iran backing down on this issue. So if the U.S. gives ultimatums, resulting in increasingly harsh sanctions, they are basically going to say, "We withdraw from the Nuclear Non-Proliferation Treaty and will go full speed ahead with our program." Then the U.S. would have to decide what they're going to do. The U.S. wouldn't be willing to lose face by backing down. The U.S. then might be tempted to escalate by saying, "Well, it will have air strikes, but they will be limited and they will not be targeting civilians. Maybe two or four days of air strikes and that's it." And, of course, the military could say it's doable. It's the job of the military to always say it's doable. The U.S. would think that is the end of it, and then Iran would have no choice but to back down.

But if Iranians are hit by air strikes, they will hit back where they have the upper hand, which is in Iraq and Afghanistan. They are obviously not going to attack the U.S., nor will they attack Israel, although people have this paranoid view about that. Iran's main strength is in Iraq and Afghanistan.

The U.S. position in both countries is weak. Iran could completely unravel it and make the quagmire in Iraq even more of a nightmare. Moqtada al-Sadr's Mahdi militia and other Iraqi Shia groups are also very dependent on Iran. If there were a Shia revolt in the south, this would really be death for the United States. There is no way the U.S. could deal with both the Sunni and the Shia revolts with 130,000 troops.

We might even be facing a major military disaster. The only way the U.S. could be able to prevent that is to send an army of another 500,000 men. And of course, to do that they would have to institute the draft. So down the line it would be a major confrontation. I don't think anyone would now say, "We're willing to do it," but the U.S. could quickly be dragged into this type of incremental escalation.

At the bottom of everything is the major, irreconcilable conflict about the nuclear issue. From the Iranian point of view, Iran has the international legal and moral right to have the whole processing cycle. The Iranians always couple this right by stating they're not interested in nuclear weapons, that they want it for civilian use, and it's their international right to have the full nuclear cycle. And in this they're correct. International agreements allow every country to have that cycle, as long as they don't develop the nuclear bomb.

The U.S. position is that under no condition can Iran be permitted to have the full nuclear cycle. In the past there was American willingness to accept Iran's having the full cycle if it didn't go ahead to the full military cycle, but this has been changed recently to the point that under no condition will the U.S. permit Iran to have this nuclear cycle. So you get an irreconcilable difference, something you cannot compromise on.

The U.S. has basically said that they're willing to use all means available to prevent Iran from having the full nuclear cycle. Iran's position is that they will continue to develop this full cycle whatever the cost. The imagery that's used in Iran is, "We are riding in a big car, driving down a one-way road, and we're going very fast. If something is in our way, it is going to get hit." Similarly, in Washington the notion is that the U.S. is going to do everything to stop Iran having the full cycle, including, of course, military strikes if necessary.

Mohamed ElBaradei, head of the International Atomic Energy Agency, and the Russians at one time suggested that Iran would be permitted to have the full cycle but not to have enough highly enriched uranium to produce bombs. There would be highly intrusive monitoring, which may have been possible for Iranians to accept. But for reasons best known to Washington, it refused to go along that way.

What are the origins of Iran's nuclear policy?

The program predates the Islamic Republic. It goes back to the 1970s, when the shah started the nuclear projects. At that time it was fully supported by the United States and Western Europe. It was even public knowledge that once you have the full nuclear cycle you can build a bomb. But there was no real concern then, and the U.S. encouraged Iran to begin its nuclear development. For a while after the revolution, the new government actually put it on a back burner.

Why is it now interested?

One major reason is national prestige. Iran feels that to be a major power it must be on the cutting edge of science. And the cutting edge of science is nuclear technology. In fact, in the editorials and discussions within the Iranian press, you will find, whether you support the government or not, whether you're a conservative or a reformer, there is general consensus that Iran has the right to have nuclear technology.

Another reason which is given, and in the West it's often pooh-poohed, is the question of energy. The argument is, since Iran is such a big oil producer, why does it need nuclear energy? Actually, economists can make a fairly good case that even a country like Iran needs energy for electricity because Iran is now actually importing a great deal of refined oil for energy. And since oil is a resource that gets depleted, it's worth preserving for future generations, when oil prices will be higher than they are now. So there is some economic argument for nuclear energy. And, of course, the U.S. and other countries are not really in a position to tell other countries that nuclear energy is an expensive way to go.

I think the most important reason for interest in nuclear energy is not necessarily the nuclear bomb, but the option of having it. The thinking of the present leadership in Iran—people who went through the Iran–Iraq war, fought in the trenches, and whose formative experience in politics was that war—[is that] the ability if ever in the same situation to resort to the option of building a bomb becomes very attractive. So even if Iran doesn't have it, [if] at some point the country is put in a corner and needs it for defensive reasons, it has this choice.

This is known in the nuclear business as the *Japanese option*. It's actually a misnomer. There are other countries in the world, approximately thirty, that have the Japanese option. It means they have the technology, the scientists, and the expertise to build it if necessary. They have the ability to assemble a bomb, but they don't build it. Let's say in the next few months North Korea actually threatens Japan with nuclear weapons. Then Japan could quickly assemble a bomb and use it as a deterrent to North Korea. Many countries have had this option for quite a while. And the Iranian leadership is thinking they would feel much more confident if they had this option at some time in the future if they needed to.

Iran has great reserves of oil and natural gas. Nevertheless, it is actually importing some petroleum products.

This isn't new. It's mainly due to lack of refining capacity and the spiraling demand for gasoline. The Iranian refineries are not able to meet internal demand. So we have the strange situation where Iran produces a lot of crude oil but it also has to import some refined oil. This situation has actually been occurring internationally over the last ten to fifteen years. There are many countries that have just overlooked the need for refining capacity. You find the same thing in the United States.

Is there much internal debate on the issue of developing nuclear energy?

Much of the country is unified on the nuclear issue; the people believe that it's their right to have nuclear energy. But on the reform-conservative side, there are distinct differences. The conservatives take a hard-line approach in terms of national security by putting more money into defense and talking tough with the United States. While the reformers, like former president Khatami, talk about dialogue of civilizations, building bridges with the West, and negotiations.

In fact, in an attempt to ease the conflict over the

nuclear issue, the previous leadership was willing to stop the nuclear process while they waited to get some sort of deal with the West. But the result of that was a U.S. "offer" that was actually sort of an insult. There was no real offer. What the Iranians wanted was for the U.S. to give up talking about regime change and offer a package to lift sanctions and permit European countries to invest in Iran. Those sorts of things would have helped the reformers to get their program through. By not offering such inducements, the U.S. actually helped the hard-liners, the conservatives. That's the main reason why in the last presidential election the hard-liners won.

What about dissidents in Iran? The best known is Nobel Prize winner Shirin Ebadi, a distinguished judge and lawyer. And there is the journalist Akbar Ganji.

There is a lot of discontent with the way the government functions and its silencing of the press. At one time there was a vibrant press with over one hundred newspapers. They acted as political parties in Iran, but they were all eventually closed down by the clerical judges. This has created a great deal of discontent.

But a point to make here is, although these dissenters criticize the government, they do not want to be identified with the Bush administration, U.S. policy with Iran, or U.S. policy in the Middle East in general. So whenever they criticize the government, they also like to distance themselves from the Bush administration. The main opposition figures—both in Iran and outside—are not playing the same role as the Iraqi opposition played against Saddam Hussein, where they actually worked very closely with the Bush administration.

People like Ahmed Chalabi and Iyad Allawi.

There really are no such figures in the Iranian opposition. Although it was hardly mentioned in the American press, the White House tried to invite some Iranian opposition figures for a meeting with Bush, and almost no one with any name was willing to accept the invitation. Even the son of the former shah found that he had a previous engagement. It actually shows the lack of credibility of the Bush administration, that even the die-hard opposition does not want to be tarnished by being associated with it. The two leading human-rights activists in Iran, Shirin Ebadi and Akbar Ganji, have made it clear that they oppose the Bush administration's policies. In order not to be identified with Washington, they have been outspoken in their criticism of the Bush administration.

Iran is a signatory to the Nuclear Non-Proliferation Treaty (NPT), and under Article 4 of that treaty it has an "inalienable right" to develop nuclear energy. Bush, on March 2, 2006, signed an agreement with India, which is not an NPT signatory, to essentially circumvent the treaty and legitimize India's nuclear weapons.

There is a lot of double-talk here, because the United States was not against Iran having nuclear energy even when it was clear in the days of the shah that he was planning for a nuclear bomb. But it didn't matter at that time, because Washington's position was that Iran was led by good guys. Now that it's not, they're in no way going to permit Iran to be anywhere near the position where they can produce a bomb.

And it's not actually inevitable that Iran would necessarily go all the way to build a bomb. What I think they want, and many of the Council of Foreign Relations people would agree, is to have the option of having a bomb. It is not necessarily in Iran's interest to have a bomb. To produce a bomb in the normal circumstances would alienate neighboring countries, would strengthen the U.S. position, and in the long run would undermine Iranian influence in the region.

I interviewed Siddharth Varadarajan, the deputy editor of the Hindu, *one of India's most prestigious English-language dailies. There is a growing demand for energy in India, and it wants to build a pipeline bringing Iranian gas and oil through Pakistan to India. He told me New Delhi has been under tremendous pressure from the U.S. not to go through with that deal, in an effort to isolate Iran economically.*

Actually, one of the rationales the U.S. gave for sharing nuclear technology with India was that India needed energy so it was going to get nuclear energy. But it would have been much easier and cheaper for Indians to get petroleum from the Middle East.

How does the 1980–88 war with Iraq influence Tehran's thinking?

For the eight years Iran fought that war, the Iraqis resorted to weapons of mass destruction—chemical warfare and gas. At that time Iran had no retaliatory ability. They relied on the international community, the UN, to pressure the Iraqis to stop using these weapons, and the UN and the international community didn't lift a finger. About half a million men were killed in the trenches, and the UN and the international community did nothing about it.

When the Iraqis first started using these weapons, the U.S. said that the Iranians were using them, too. And then when the Iranian casualties showed up in Europe for medical attention, they became even more cynical. They said the Iranians were using them on their own troops to discredit the Iraqis. Then when the Iraqis used these weapons against the Kurds and the Halabja massacre happened [in March 1988], Washington claimed that it was the Iranians that had used them on the Kurds, not the Iraqis. The U.S. didn't come around to blaming Saddam Hussein for the use of poison gas until later. To be more precise, three days after Saddam Hussein became a bad guy and invaded Kuwait in August 1990, suddenly the State Department found conclusive evidence that Saddam Hussein had used gas in Halabja years earlier and had used lethal chemicals and mustard gas against Iran. This was years after the fact.

Then when the U.S. was talking about invading Iraq in 2002–3, the whole story was again revived, leaving out the part that these weapons had all actually come from western countries. And, of course, when the term *evil* was used to refer to Saddam Hussein because he had used chemical weapons on his own people, the Kurds, there was very little mention of their use on Iranians.

It's because of that experience that Iranian leaders feel that if there is a war against them in the future, they will not be able to rely on international morality or international influence for protection. They constantly say that they need to be independent and self-reliant, which basically means the ability, if need be, to produce a weapon of deterrence if confronted by a similar situation.

You could argue, then, that if they're really that concerned about the nuclear option, why don't they go full speed ahead and actually build the bomb quickly in order to have it now. Here again, you can think of rational reasons why it doesn't make sense for them to have a bomb in the near future. You can actually see it in the discussions in the Iranian newspapers. It's the only case I know of in international politics where a country has actually discussed the pros and cons of building a bomb. Other countries developed the bomb secretly— including the United States and Britain—for obvious reasons, but in Iran there has actually been a discussion whether this is a good road to go down or not.

You will find fairly conservative people from the military arguing against having the nuclear option. For instance, at one point the minister of defense argued that it would not be in the interests of Iran to have a bomb. And the reason he gave is this: if Iran actually had a bomb, it would scare the hell out of small Arab states in the near vicinity and they would become more pro-American. This would undermine Iranian influence and prestige in the neighborhood, which is obviously something they don't want to do and would not be in the best interests of Iranian national security.

Another argument is that having a bomb is not

much of a deterrent if the U.S. is in the game. So if you're fighting a country such as Iraq or some other neighboring country, the option of having a nuclear bomb is worthwhile, but having a few bombs against the U.S. is no real deterrent. Interestingly enough, this is the main reason Saddam Hussein gave up the bomb. Saddam Hussein's main nuclear scientist was interviewed and asked, Why did Saddam Hussein not pursue it? He said, Saddam Hussein basically told us, what's the point of having a bomb if you're only going to fight the U.S.? What are you going to do, drop a bomb on a U.S. base in Kuwait? And then the U.S. will come and bomb twenty cities in Iraq. So it's not really an equal situation where you can use it as a deterrent. And I'm sure the Iranian military leaders think along the same lines.

So when Iran says they're not interested in the bomb, I would not dismiss this as pure propaganda. They would have good reasons not to be interested in the bomb in the near future. Iran's supreme leader and other clerics have said that the bomb is un-Islamic and there is a fatwa from Khamenei that they shouldn't build the bomb.

Hundreds of thousands of Iranians were killed and many more wounded in the war between Iran and Iraq.

It's estimated that Iran lost about half a million men fighting. The chemicals and mustard gas did not cause most of the casualties. Most of the casualties were in trench warfare, conventional fighting. In fact, mustard gas turned out to be inefficient, and often Saddam Hussein's troops suffered in using the stuff because it's very unreliable.

What role does the 1979–80 hostage crisis play in U.S. calculations? Is there some payback factor at work?

The hostage crisis plays a residual role in that some American politicians would like to "get even." But I don't think that it determines policy. After all, Reagan and some of the neoconservatives were more than eager to deal with Tehran during the Irangate scandal. The hostage crisis also remains in the memory of the American public and can be tapped into by the administration if it chooses to do so. It is like a tap that can be turned on or off. If the U.S. goes for air strikes, we will see replays of the 1979–80 television tapes of the hostage crisis. If not, they could be dismissed as ancient history. After all, the United States often tells Iran to forget about the 1953 coup, on the grounds that it is all ancient history.

For the neoconservatives, the disaster in the Middle East was the 1979 revolution. And they have not hidden the fact that they really want to undo that revolution, which means regime change. They want to put the clock back to the good old days when the government in Iran was very pro-American. That is their underlying agenda. But I don't think the neocons are so much in the driver's seat now.

Is the memory of the 1953 coup that overthrew the democratically elected government of Mohammed Mossadegh a factor in Tehran's calculations?

Very much so. The CIA carried out the 1953 coup, and therefore, anyone in Iran who is seen as close to the U.S. is then also seen as part of a coup conspiracy.

Are there any alternative positions in the U.S. establishment toward Iran?

There have been proposals made, especially from the Council on Foreign Affairs in their journal *For-*

eign Affairs [March/April 2005]. The article "Taking on Tehran" was written by two experts on Iran, Ray Takeyh and Kenneth Pollack. The latter, a former Clinton official, was a strong advocate for the Iraq war. They assert that if the U.S. provided the right conditions, Iran could have been brought into negotiations to give full proof, and that this would have guaranteed that they would not develop a bomb. They also spell out certain conditions to support the moderates, who would then be able to guarantee that there would not be the full nuclear process necessary for making a bomb.

But the U.S. has not followed those conditions and has, in fact, knocked them down. Instead, the U.S. position has been to up the ante and put pressure on Iran. U.S. Ambassador to the UN John R. Bolton made the argument at the UN that Iran would be given thirty days to respond to the mild UN resolution about stopping its nuclear research. Bolton says if Iran does not stop it, then it will go into Chapter 7, which is a major resolution. If Iran is then in violation of a major UN resolution, the ball starts rolling down the hill and you have a resemblance with the crisis in Iraq.

Some of the rhetoric we've been hearing is that

Iran is an expansionist power, Iran is a totalitarian state, and that Iran is the mother of all terrorism. Some of the neoconservatives have been [saying] for quite some time that the U.S. is in the midst of World War IV, World War III being the Cold War. In this World War IV, the U.S.'s main antagonist is Iran. People like Victor Hanson, whose work seems to be Cheney's main bedside reading, has been arguing that Iran and the U.S. are in a mortal, life-and-death struggle; one side has to win, the other side has to lose. In this type of rhetoric, there is obviously no room for negotiations.

In fact, this type of rhetoric sabotages any type of negotiations, because while the Council on Foreign Relations and the more pragmatic conservatives in Washington talk about negotiations and trying to persuade Iranians to not go whole hog, one side is talking about the destruction of the Islamic Republic. And you really can't go into a negotiating room with a gun, saying that you're going to shoot at the first opportunity. The other side probably will come to the room with the same type of weapon, and you're more likely to get a shoot-out than negotiations. The U.S. also had this type of negotiating with North Korea. Clinton was doing a fairly good job negotiating with North Korea, but the Republicans argued that this was a sellout and that they were never going to negotiate with the U.S.—the term they used was "a pygmy." Not surprisingly, when Bush came into power, the North Koreans pulled out of the Nuclear Non-Proliferation Treaty and went ahead with their nuclear program. The rhetoric itself can determine policy, speed up the tempo, and lead to further escalation.

Iran's political structure is unusual in that there is a secular formation running parallel to a sectarian one.

The Iranian constitution is very complicated. Condoleezza Rice dismisses it as totalitarian. In fact, it is in many ways pluralistic. I would call it an oligarchical system where there are different centers of power. There is no real concentration of overwhelming power in one person or one institution. The major reason for this complexity is due to Khomeini and the authors of the constitution, who tried, after the revolution, to merge two very different philosophies of government. One was the western philosophy of popular sovereignty and democracy; the other was Khomeini's own version of clerical theocracy, which ultimately gave the clergy the power to interpret religious law.

Ultimately the question became: where does power reside, in the people—the sovereignty of the masses—or in the religious experts? And the way the constitution was designed was to bring in these two incompatible philosophies. So there is a mixture of popular sovereignty and clerical sovereignty in the constitution.

What role does the supreme leader, Ayatollah Ali Khamenei, play politically?

The president, as the head of the executive branch, presides over the cabinet. But he is not a presidential authority as in ordinary republics, because ultimately the supreme leader can overrule the president. The supreme leader makes many crucial appointments, such as commanders in chief, heads of radio and television networks, and the directors of big religious foundations, which are very important positions. The supreme leader also has the constitutional role of guiding—the term that is used is *guiding*—the Islamic Republic, so he can overrule the president on key issues, if necessary. When it comes to presidential elections, he can vet the candidates. So sovereignty here is split between the president and the supreme leader but is mostly enjoyed by the latter.

The supreme leader is technically elected. He is elected by something like an electoral college of eighty-six people known as the Assembly of Experts, who are in turn elected by the general electorate. But it's not as if anyone can run for the Assembly of Experts. You have to be vetted. Usually only clerics run. It becomes like a college of cardinals: they choose who is to be the supreme leader. Technically, they can remove the supreme leader if they feel he is no longer able to carry out his functions. So even the supreme leader here does not have ultimate or absolute power. He can be removed.

In short, one could describe the political system in Iran as both republican and Islamic. It is republican in that most high officials are elected. But it is also Islamic in that these high officials are supposed to be subordinate to Islamic law, *sharia*, and clerics decide what is in conformity with Islamic law.

Is there anything in Shia doctrine that delineates this singular political system in Iran?

It's often said this comes from Shiism. In fact, it's a novel idea. It's Khomeini's theory of government. He packaged it as very traditional Shiism, but in fact it's very much a break from Shia tradition. In the past in Shiism, religious leaders had authority to basically guide the people, but that didn't extend to political guidance; it meant guidance in terms of law. Often the religious leader's authority was guidance over individuals who were incapable of running their own affairs, such as orphans, the mentally incapacitated, and widows. They were basically put under the guidance of the *mujtahids*, the religious leaders.

But what Khomeini did was he politicized the whole concept of what is called *vilayat-e faqih*, the authority of the religious leaders. So in many ways this is a twentieth-century invention; it's not deep-rooted in Shia theory going back centuries.

Talk about Mahmoud Ahmadinejad.

Ahmadinejad is the president. He's elected by the general electorate. He is a layman; previous presidents have been clerics. From 1997 until 2005, while Iran was led by Khatami, a reformist moderate, there was a good chance of having rapprochement with the U.S. The problems mainly came from Washington. And now that there is a hard-liner in the presidency in Iran, it's sort of a mirror image. Ahmadinejad is not very different from Bush in terms of style, rhetoric, and mentality. The only difference is he's more of a genuine populist. He comes from the working class; he lives a modest life. This is one of the cachets he has for getting votes.

What was the importance of Bush's naming Iran as an "axis of evil" state, in his 2002 State of the Union address?

Bush's naming Iran as a member of the "axis of evil" was a major blunder if the U.S. was at all concerned with helping the democratic movement in Iran. The reformers in Iran, such as President Khatami, were seen as favoring improved relations with the United States. As soon as President Bush denounced Iran as "evil" and started using threatening language, the rug was pulled out from under the reformers. Some reformers became vociferously anti-U.S. Some remained silent. Some withdrew from active politics. This all helped in diminishing the reform vote in the last presidential election and thereby in bringing victory to Ahmadinejad.

And he defeated a cleric, Ali Akbar Hashemi Rafsanjani.

Yes, and Rafsanjani was running as a moderate. Besides Rafsanjani, in the first round of elections there were other moderates who split the vote. They were the real heirs to the previous president, Khatami, who had twice won landslide victories. But the huge reform electorate both eroded and splintered. I would say the main reason for erosion was the axis-of-evil speech, because that was a slap in the face to the reformers. Many reformers in that last election either stayed home or felt that national security was the most important issue and voted with the hard-liners.

Have there been instances where the supreme leader has overruled the president?

Khomeini often did that. In fact, he dismissed the first president of Iran after the revolution, Abolhassan Bani-Sadr, because there was a direct clash between the two. Khomeini basically told the *majlis* to take away his power. That's what they did, and Bani-Sadr found himself in exile in Paris.

Why is the U.S. confronting Iran at this time?

Here you find both sides feel that they are in a good position. Both sides feel overconfident. And this is where a lot of the misjudgment comes. Both sides feel that they can play chicken with the other side because they have the trump card.

What advantages does the U.S. feel it has?

One thing is that in the last year the U.S. has been able to get the Europeans on board. So it's not the United States, or the neocons, against Iran; it's Europe and the U.S. isolating Iran from the international community. This boosts Washington's confidence. In addition to this, there is the American political foreign-policy elite, who are pretty much united here. It's not just a neocon issue. Others, including Democrats, are fearful of Iran's nuclear program. And there is potential of getting people like liberal Democrats as gung ho about strong actions against Iran as are the usual suspects in Washington.

Another card that the U.S. feels it has is an alliance with third-world countries such as India and Brazil. So in the voting at the UN over the nuclear issue, you find that these other countries vote along with the United States. This gives people like Bolton the feeling that they are in a good position to pressure Iran at the UN. In fact, whenever one of the sides feels it has the upper hand, it feels unmoved to negotiate because it thinks that the other side is going to cave in. We now know that right after the U.S. invaded Iraq and took Baghdad, the Iranians were willing to negotiate. They sent offers to negotiate and Washington refused to pursue them, probably because the U.S. felt that everything was going their way in Iraq. Why should they negotiate with those whom they were planning to target next?

Another thing that gives the U.S. confidence is its huge military power. The $500 billion it spends on the military gives the U.S. Air Force and Navy the ability to strike at Iran, and Iran's military capabilities are basically nothing in comparison. So Washington sees this as an important trump card, which it can always use.

What about the Iranian side?

Iranian leaders, including the president and the supreme leader, feel that they have the upper hand. They feel they have the U.S. where they want it. Why? One major reason is that they have full confidence over controlling their own society. They can mobilize the public behind the flag on the nuclear issue. They know that as soon as there is a military strike on Iran, the public is going to rally around them. People who even criticized the regime before are going to basically pursue a policy of self-censorship. Only crazy people are going to openly criticize the regime at a time of national danger, being a threat from the U.S. So nothing would rally the public around the regime more than a military confrontation with the United States.

Another misperception in Washington is that somehow Iran is like Eastern Europe or Serbia, that the regime can be overthrown through destabilization and regime change. Some crazy people in Washington have been running workshops in the Persian Gulf trying to train Iranians on how to demonstrate, as if the Iranians need someone to teach them how to demonstrate. The idea that Iran is somehow like Poland or Serbia or Ukraine is bizarre. The whole history of the country and the experience are so different.

The U.S. Congress has recently given $85 million to Iranian dissidents to destabilize the regime. All this does is fuel the Iranian perception that the U.S. is not really interested in negotiations; they're only interested in the overthrow of the regime. But they're not actually worried about the $85 million. For the Iranians, that's seen as money down the rat hole. Iranian émigrés might take advantage of this, but it's certainly not going to cause a problem in Iran.

The main reason Iran now feels confident is Iraq. Because of its quagmire in Iraq, the U.S. is now caught up in the hands of Iran, whether it likes it or not. The three main Iraqi Shiite groups are very much dependent on Iran. Even the one that was least dependent on Iran is becoming more allied with Iran. So far, Iran has used its influence to help stabilize the situation. Both the U.S. and Iran want a stable government in Baghdad. Even though the U.S. and Iran have different interests on other issues, where Iraq is concerned they are pursuing similar goals. Without Iranian support, the U.S. situation in Iraq would have been much worse.

So the Iranians know that if there is a crisis with the U.S., all they have to do is give a green light to the Iraqis—especially Sadr—who are itching to fight with the United States. The Iranians don't even have to supply Sadr with weapons. He has the weapons. All they have to do is tell him, "We're no longer restraining you. Do whatever you want."

If you actually follow what's happening on the ground in Iraq, you will see how precarious the U.S. position is in Baghdad. Baghdad could be easily surrounded, cut off. You're not talking about basically an insurgency limited to the Sunni area. An insurgency in the Shia area would make the nightmarish situation for the U.S. far more nightmarish.

So these are the most important cards the Iranians feel they have. But there is another one, which is often mentioned in the press here, the oil card. Iranians have made it clear they're not going to use the oil card, mainly because they depend on imports of oil and they need oil exports for their income. Any type of escalation of the crisis is going to lead to a major spike in oil prices. Prices are currently $60 a barrel. They could very well jump up to $100 a barrel, which would probably be the right price or a just price for oil, but I don't think the average American consumer would consider it just. That's a factor to be taken into account as the polemics increase.

Since both sides have trump cards, what we're seeing is both sides playing the game of chicken. They are both trying to intimidate the other side to back down and feeling that if the other side is rational, they will figure that it's better to moderate and back down, rather than go to the brink. The trouble with this is that neither side seems capable of backing down because of the positions they've already taken, because of public image, and because of their own internal constituencies. The U.S. attitude has been that if it talks tough, the result will be the Iranians coming to their senses and saying, "Well, we don't want to be hit by this major power, and therefore we will back down and give up the policy of having the full cycle."

The Sadr you mentioned is Moqtada al-Sadr, son of a respected Shia cleric. When he visited Iran he said that if it were to be attacked by the U.S., his militia would fight against the Americans in Iraq. U.S. hostility toward Iran is nothing new. The 1979 revolution, which overthrew the U.S. ally and satrap, the shah, was a major blow to U.S. power in the Middle East. Essentially, there have been a few moments of better relations. The first was during the Iran-Contra affair, when Robert McFarland, Reagan's national security adviser, went to Tehran in 1986 with a cake for Khomeini, and the second was during the attack on Afghanistan in 2001. Except for those two examples, it's been negative.

What is Iran's relationship with the political parties that are now dominating in Iraq, specifically the SCIRI (Supreme Council for the Islamic Revolution in Iraq) and the Dawa Party?

There are three Shia parties: those two you mentioned, and there is Moqtada Sadr's militia, *Jesh al-Mahdi*. The Dawa and SCIRI took shelter in Iran when Saddam Hussein forced them out of Iraq. They were given refuge and were helped financially and militarily. In fact, SCIRI had quite a large militia in Iran, which fought with Iran against Saddam Hussein.

That's the Badr brigade.

Yes, they are very closely tied to Iran. So when Saddam Hussein's regime collapsed, Dawa and SCIRI were well placed to have influence in Baghdad. The irony here is that the American occupation of Iraq brings two groups that were pro-Iranian to power. So Iran and the U.S. seem to be working on parallel tracks here, because they're both supporting the same people in Baghdad. The leaders of Dawa were, until recently, on the wanted list by the FBI for trying to blow up the American embassy in Kuwait. A few years ago they were known as international terrorists, and now they are accepted in the White House as great leaders of the emerging democracy in Iraq. You could say the U.S. reliance on Dawa and SCIRI is very tenuous, because the U.S. knows that these two organizations are much closer ideologically to Iran than to the United States.

The third group is led by Moqtada al-Sadr. Ironically, in the past he was the most critical of Iran. He actually made some derogatory statements about Iran and Iranians after Saddam Hussein fell. He felt that people who had Iranian citizenship should not be interfering in Iraqi politics. The reason for this was that Iran was supporting Dawa and SCIRI. But in the last year, Sadr has become more vociferous and anti-American, and as the relations between Iran and the U.S. deteriorate, Sadr is building bridges with Iran. He could very well be a major threat to the U.S. if the U.S. carries out air strikes against Iran. Iran would not even have to give a green light to Sadr and other Shia groups; Iran would just turn off the red light and basically let nature run its course in Iraq. I think you would get a major Shia revolt against the U.S., led by Sadr.

The senior clerical figure in Iraq is Ayatollah Sistani, who is Iranian. What kind of relations does he have with Tehran?

He was not involved in politics in the past, but he is by default being dragged in because of the U.S. invasion. During the whole revolutionary situation in Iran, his name never appeared. He was separate from all the political ayatollahs. His Iranian nationality really doesn't play a role in this. Sistani is considered someone who is more of a scholar who likes to act as an adviser behind the scenes. He doesn't want a clerical republic. This doesn't mean that he opposes clerics having influence. Whatever happens in Iraq, clerics, including himself, are going to have a lot of influence. So if he tells people to vote or not to vote, or tells them to come out into the streets, he is acting as a political leader as well as a clerical leader.

One term that's gaining some currency is the Shia crescent. *Explain what that is.*

This fits into the narrative that Iran is a major threat and that Iran is a Shia state capable of controlling all the Shias in the region. Of course, there are Shias in Iraq; there are Shias in Lebanon; there are some Shias in Saudi Arabia, in Bahrain, in other places in the Gulf, as well as Pakistan and Afghanistan, but that does not mean that Iran is going to export an anti-American, anti-Israeli revolution through Shiism. Again, this presupposes that Iran controls all these different Shia populations, that there is an international Shia movement like international communism. The various Shia groups in Iraq also have their own interests, and they're not beholden to Iran. They might receive help from Iran when they need it, but they're not creatures of Iran.

It turns out that when there was a minor Shia revolt in 2003, when Sadr had his uprising, the situation in the Green Zone became so serious that

[L. Paul] Bremer was even thinking of imposing food rationing on American officials there. What does that mean? If you have a huge U.S. army there, they are dependent on supplies, and those supply lines go through Shia regions. If the Shias start an uprising, you're talking about a nightmarish situation such as the Berlin Blockade, or maybe even a situation such as a Dien Bien Phu. The Shias have that capability, since most of the southern areas and half of Baghdad are under Shia control. The only reason Shia areas have been fairly quiet since the invasion is because the British, especially in the south, handed over local control lock, stock, and barrel to Shia organizations. These entities would be very susceptible to Iranian influence now. So I think the Iranian position is [that] there is not much the U.S. can do on the nuclear issue because if they do anything, Iran is in a position to hit the U.S. really hard in Iraq.

Afghanistan and Pakistan are on Iran's eastern borders, and in both there are insurgencies. In Pakistan there is an uprising in its western province of Baluchistan, and in Afghanistan the Taliban are resurgent.

The Kabul government was set up by the U.S. with the help of Iran because of Iran's common interest with the U.S. to get rid of the Taliban and al-Qaeda. Without Iranian support behind the scenes to get the warlords to cooperate with [Hamid] Karzai, the Kabul government would never have been set up. They exerted their influence, pressuring both the warlords and the Northern Alliance to cooperate and set up the Kabul government. So far the warlords are basically dealing with Karzai, but there are plenty of warlords that are itching to go their own way. One warlord, Gulbuddin Hekmatyar, who was actually pro-Iranian, refused to go with the Iranian advice. He went off to the mountains and is obviously causing problems there. Again, all they need from Iran is a green light and the U.S. position in Afghanistan could also unravel.

I think in Afghanistan, what Iran does in the future very much depends on what the U.S. does in Iran. If there is an escalation and war, Iran would do in Afghanistan what it will do in Iraq, which is make life miserable for the United States. So they could easily give a green light to the warlords, arm people like Hekmatyar, and the whole place would unravel. The situation in Afghanistan is pretty desperate. The Afghan government is really no more than the mayorship of Kabul. If you go outside Kabul, the central government has no authority at all. The warlords are in control.

And Pakistan?

I can't speak in detail about Pakistan, but clearly in the last elections, Islamicist groups won in two of the four provinces. The central government has probably lost more support since then. The deal which Bush made with India hardly helps [Pakistani president Pervez] Musharraf. So if things unravel there, it would be much worse a situation for the U.S. than Iran and its nuclear policy, because Pakistan already has nuclear weapons, and it wouldn't be in anyone's interest for terrorist groups to have those weapons.

Ahmadinejad threatened to wipe Israel off the map. Why is he making those kinds of comments?

I think it's reflective of his own way of thinking. The right-wing conservatives in Iran, like the world over, have a fairly narrow perspective of history. What

Amadinejad would read in his newspapers, which are right-wing newspapers, would be Holocaust denial and anti-Jewish sentiment. So that's there.

He harps on it because it's a way of bridging the gap between Shiism and Sunnism and Iranism and Arabism. Iran has always felt that it's peripheral to Middle East politics. And with the Iraqi crisis in the Arab world, Iran is ironically seen as cooperating with the United States. From the U.S. perspective this seems absurd, but from a Sunni perspective, there is a government in Baghdad, it's Shia, it's pro-Iranian, but it's also being supported by the United States. So the view is that there is some sort of funny conspiracy going on here.

I think because both Iran and the U.S. have so far have wanted a stable government in Baghdad; they've ended up backing the same horses. By making this pitch for Arab support on the issue of Palestine and Israel, Amadinejad is saying to the Arab world, "I am at the forefront of the struggle against Zionism, and your Arab leaders are spineless. They don't speak for the Muslim world, but we speak for the Muslim world." It's a way of trying to bridge that gap.

*Does this resonate among the general Iranian popula-
tion? Iran is a non-Arab country; it's not contiguous
geographically with Palestine.*

I don't think it resonates much in Iran, only among
the die-hards. But it resonates well on the Arab
street. And I think that's where he's targeting.
Within Iran, especially among reformers, the idea
is that although they have sympathy for the Palestinian cause, they feel they should support it rather
than get immersed in it. Khatami, the previous
president, said that they would support any decision
the Palestinians made. So if the Palestinians wanted
a two-state solution under Arafat, they were quite
happy to go along with it. Some conservative
diehards viewed that as a betrayal of *sharia*. However, Khamenei has said Iran would agree to
whatever the Palestinians decide.

What about Hamas?

The victory of Hamas gives the Iranian leadership
some leeway, because before they had no influence
with the PLO and Arafat. There was a great deal of
strain between them. Iran is much more in tune

with Hamas. And if the Europeans and Americans carry out their threats to cut off all aid, I wouldn't be surprised if Iran steps in and shames all the Arab countries by offering aid. This would be seen as a major extension of Iranian influence in the region.

What are Iran's relations with Hezbollah in Lebanon?

They have been close. Iran helped Hezbollah get off the ground after the Israelis occupied Lebanon in 1982. It has sent a lot of money and equipment. At one time it used to train Hezbollah fighters. I don't think this is still the case, but at one time Iran had revolutionary guards in Lebanon helping Hezbollah. There are also a great deal of family connections; many of the clerics in Iran have relatives in Lebanon. This goes back to the sixteenth and seventeenth centuries. There is a long history of links between the Shias in Lebanon and Shias in Iran.

Having said that, one has to also stress that Hezbollah is not an instrument of Iran. Hezbollah is very much an independent group. Its leaders make their own decisions, and they're not really beholden to Iran. Hezbollah has its own interest, which is to preserve itself, and it doesn't take orders from anyone else, especially from Iran. They would accept Iranian advice, they would accept Iranian help, but in terms of orders, that's something that would be unacceptable for Hezbollah. And I think the Iranians are sophisticated enough not to think in those terms.

The recent crisis in Lebanon was seen as an American victory, but the net result after all the dust settled was that Hezbollah had increased its influence and its membership in the parliament and for the first time got members in the cabinet. Because the Syrians were forced out of Lebanon, Hezbollah has become more dependent on Iran than it was before. Before, it relied much more on Syria.

Is the connection that Tehran has with Hezbollah based on theological grounds, or is there some geopolitical component, as well?

I think it is mostly its historical connections. Since the revolution there have been strong ties. The idea that Iran aspires to be a major power with intentions of rebuilding the old Iranian empire from the Mediterranean to India [comes from] the wild imaginations of people in Washington. Iranian leaders are more down-to-earth. They realize Iran has limited power. It's really a Gulf State power, not a Mediterranean power. It doesn't have a reach to the Mediterranean.

And I think the idea that Iran could use Hezbollah to threaten Israel is off the wall. They would help Hezbollah in defending Lebanon and use Hezbollah in terms of propaganda to support the Palestinian cause, but in terms of a practical instrument to threaten Israel, that's really not in the cards. One major mistake the Israelis are making is thinking that Hezbollah is so closely tied to Iran that once the U.S. attacks Iran, Iran would automatically use Hezbollah against Israel. I don't think that's in the works.

How has the Israeli attack on Lebanon changed the equation?

Much has been said about Israel's war against Lebanon in July and August 2006. I don't think it has changed Iranian policy. The Iranian government never placed much stress on Hezbollah as deterrence on Israel, knowing well that the latter had overwhelming firepower in the region. Iran's

main strength has been in Iraq and Afghanistan—
not in Lebanon.

This type of premise in Washington completely
ignores Iranian history. Iranian history for the last
150 years has been a history of having to struggle
with foreign imperialism. And in that history, the
imperial powers, particularly Britain, were constantly giving ultimatums to Iran. In Iranian
history, Iranian politicians who submitted to ultimatums are considered national traitors, and the
national leaders who refuse to submit are invariably
considered heroes. Even if they lost, they've been
considered heroes.

So the present crisis in Iran is being seen as a
replay of the oil nationalization crisis with
Mossadegh, and Iranians are drawing parallels to
Iran in 1951–53, when Iran wanted to be a self-suf-
ficient, self-respecting nation and have sovereignty
over its resources. The Americans and the British
offered these ultimatums: if you don't give up your
oil, we're going to destroy you. And Mossadegh was
a hero; even though he didn't succeed, he stood up
for national rights.

Iranians are seeing a similar thing, except now
it's the question of nuclear technology. If you look

back to the early twentieth century, a partial myth in Iranian historiography is that Iran couldn't develop railways because British and Russian imperialism wouldn't allow it. Every time Iran wanted to build railways, which was at that time the cutting edge of technology, the imperial powers stepped in and said, "No, you're not good enough, you're not developed enough to have railways." This now plays into the question of nuclear technology, the argument being that Iran really doesn't need it or Iran isn't mature enough to have nuclear technology.

Ariel Sharon, whom George Bush called a "man of peace" when he was prime minister, urged the U.S. to go after Iran "the day after Iraq is crushed." Well, Iraq is a slight problem.

Some of the neocons felt that Iran was the real enemy, not Saddam Hussein.

There was some line like "Real men go to Tehran."

I think when Jay Garner, the first American proconsul, came back, Bush asked him, "Are you ready to invade Iran?" And his response was, "I'd rather invade Cuba first." So these guys seem to have a long list of countries they want to invade.

Is the war talk from Washington serious?

In Washington there is a big debate at the moment about whether the bellicose talk is serious or not. The most benign interpretation you can give is that this talk is a part of the bargaining process; if you threaten the other side, they're more likely to listen to you, but you're not actually planning to follow through with your threats. The problem with this is, once you start using the language, you eventually become committed to it. If the other side doesn't back down, the discourse then determines policy, because then you can't turn around and say, "Well, I never really said those things. I didn't really mean it." If you don't act, you appear to be chickening out and then not behaving as a superpower, as a big, macho power, which is important in Washington. So, what you find is the language itself can lead the policy.

It's often hard to take State Department or administration officials seriously when they're in a position of authority, because they're talking only about what is official. Here I'd like to quote something that came out on April 6, 2006, from Wayne White, a former State Department official. Here's a man who spent his whole time actually doing intelligence work for the State Department. He's no longer there, so he's a free person. He says, "In recent months I have grown increasingly concerned that the administration has been giving thought to a heavy dose of air strikes against Iran's nuclear sector without giving enough weight to the possible ramifications of such action." Here is someone in the know who is saying that they've been talking about this, but now he's really concerned that the talk could be serious and that the administration really doesn't think beyond the strikes or about the ramifications.

So action against Iran is being packaged as limited air strikes with no so-called collateral damage. It would be maybe two, three, four days. But after four days it will basically be settled. The nuclear installations will be destroyed, and the U.S. would have achieved what it wanted. What isn't being calculated is the retaliation from the other side. This is typical imperial hubris, as if the other side doesn't exist or doesn't have options it can take, as well.

U.S. actions have their consequences, which are usually forgotten or ignored. Similar to Iraq, very few people are giving warning of consequences once the U.S. has taken action. With Iraq, voices opposing the war were relegated to the fringes of the debate. Again, the danger is not seriously discussed. What are the consequences? Even if it was a successful four-day surgical strike, even if the U.S. was one hundred percent successful in removing these installations, which will be very hard because they are most likely hidden, nuclear material may be dispersed, air strikes may not succeed, it may even lead Iran to accelerate toward not just the nuclear cycle but the full development of the bomb.

The consequence, which is not openly discussed but the U.S. military would quickly become very aware of, is that Iran would retaliate. They're not going to attack Israel over Lebanon. The Iranian position is much weaker. They're not going to openly challenge the U.S. Air Force or Navy in the Gulf. The rational thing for Iran to do, if there are air strikes, is basically do nothing but quietly give a green light to the Iraqi Shias and the warlords in Afghanistan.

And then, with an unraveling of the U.S. situation in those two countries, the U.S. will enter a full-blown war in the Middle East. Then we're faced with the question, is the U.S. willing to send an army of, let's say, a million soldiers to stabilize the situation in those countries and institute a draft in order to recruit and sustain that number of troops?

So what we're seeing is a typical case of policy makers making incremental decisions, thinking that one decision is going to solve the problem. The problem is that these decisions would escalate things. And before you know it, we're going to be in the midst of a major war, like with the Schlieffen Plan in 1914 or with Hitler's invasion of Poland. The U.S. may be entering a type of war that was not originally planned. The neocons wouldn't plan this, but it would be a gradual drift into this type of situation. The other side is as adamant as America is about what its rights and interests are, and they're as unlikely to buckle under as the people in Washington.

Neocon advocates for regime change in Iran say that Azeris, Kurds, and Arabs, who constitute about 45 percent of the country's population, are ripe for exploitation and manipulation in fostering upheaval. What is the likelihood of that happening?

The neoconservatives have introduced something new in U.S.–Iran relations: the ethnic card. Ever since 1941, when the U.S. got involved in Iranian politics, it has supported the national integrity of Iran and its central government. By changing course, the U.S. is fishing in troubled waters. There is some legitimate discontent among some of the ethnic minorities, but it is not to the extent that could unravel Iran. Many of the non-Persian communities are well integrated—especially in economic terms—into the larger state. Many of them speak and write in Persian—thanks to the successful anti-illiteracy campaigns waged since the revolution. Resorting to the ethnic card also puts off the vast majority of Iranians. This partly explains why the son of the shah did not accept an invitation to the White House recently. He didn't want to be there with nonentities who claimed to represent persecuted ethnic minorities. Of course, in much of the Middle East, people will see the U.S. resort to the ethnic card as being in the long imperialist tradition of divide and rule. After more than three years of American occupation, Iraq has become a nightmare due to communal violence—something that did not exist before. The U.S. is also using the same tactic in Lebanon by claiming that Hezbollah is not really Lebanese because it is Shia. The U.S. is doing this throughout the region, focusing on Sunni–Shia differences and claiming that there is such a thing as a "Shia crescent" threatening not only Israel and the U.S., but also the Sunni world. Historians of nineteenth-century imperialism would find these tactics familiar.

What would it take for a rapprochement between Iran and the United States?

It would have to be a full deal where the U.S. agrees that they're not interested in regime change and that they accept Iran as an important power in the Gulf. They would have to lift sanctions, not prevent other countries from investing in Iran, and Iran, in return, would have to give some guarantees. I don't mean verbal guarantees, but guarantees that its nuclear program is not designed to produce nuclear bombs.

3

Culture and Resistance: Writing Back to Power
NAHID MOZAFFARI

Describe your work with PEN [poets, playwrights, essayists, editors, and novelists] American Center.

I'm a historian by training, but I have also studied Iranian literature and know a number of poets and writers. Since the early 1990s I've been working with PEN on matters relating to writers and publishers in Iran. Throughout those years, the government was cracking down on writers, journalists, and intellectuals who were at the forefront of the pressures for change. I came across a lot of cases of writers who were imprisoned, disappeared, or killed. Later we found out that the serial murders were carried out by security agents connected to the Iranian Ministry of Information. So my focus became worrying about what was happening to writers and intellectuals, as well keeping up with literary production and trends.

In 1999, PEN and Columbia University arranged for some Iranian writers to visit New York. We realized that their American counterparts and readers knew very little about the contemporary literary scene in Iran. In a sense, [Iranian writers] are treated as human-rights guinea pigs when they come here. The Iranians appreciated the attention to the difficulties they face, but they also wanted to be known as writers. They wanted their work to be considered as part of world literature, to be discussed and critiqued. PEN had a project called the "threatened literatures series" at that time. That's how this project of compiling and publishing *Strange Times, My Dear*, an anthology of some of the best fiction and poetry written in Iran since the 1979 revolution, was conceived. It was especially important that this book would be accessible to the general English-speaking reader and not only to scholars and specialists.

Explain the title of your book.

It comes from a line from a poem, written shortly after the revolution, called "In This Blind Alley," by Ahmad Shamlu. He was one of the most revered lit-

erary figures in modern Iranian history and a highly
regarded oppositional poet. Shamlu remained in
Iran from the revolution until his death in the summer of 2000 and continued to write despite
continuous harassment by the regime. My American friends are amazed when I tell them that tens
of thousands—some say one hundred thousand
people—showed up in tribute for his funeral pro-
cession in Tehran. Let me read part of the poem. (It
was translated by Ahmad Karimi-Hakkak.)

> *They smell your breath lest you have said: I*
>   *love you.*
>   *They smell your heart:*
>   *These are strange times, my dear.*
> *They flog love*
> *at the roadblock.*
> *Let's hide love in the larder.*
>
> *In this crooked blind alley, as the chill descends*
> *they feed fires*
> *with logs of song and poetry*
> *Hazard not a thought:*
>   *These are strange times, my dear.*

The man who knocks at your door in the noon
*   of the night*
has come to kill the light.
*   Let's hide light in the larder.*

There, butchers are posted in passageways
with bloody chopping blocks and cleavers:
*   These are strange times, my dear.*

They chop smiles off lips,
and songs off the mouth:
Let's hide joy in the larder.

Shamlu builds the image of the gradually creeping control of the religious factions over the revolution by showing how song, poetry, and love itself had to be hidden from the authorities. "Larder" symbolizes a closed space.

Most westerners, if they have any knowledge of Iranian literature, it's pretty much limited to the classical Sufi poetry of Rumi and perhaps Hafez. Who are some of the major voices today that we should know about?

Among the older generation, there are still some writers that were already well established before the revolution. They have written poignantly about the injustices of poverty, the displacement that accompanies massive social flux, the ambiguities and uncertainties of political ideologies, and the brutalities of war. The prominent ones are Mahmoud Dowlatabadi; Hushang Golshiri, who died in 2000; Esmail Fassih; Simin Daneshvar; and various others.

After the Iranian revolution and the war with Iraq (1980–88), a younger cohort began to emerge, and women writers began to stand out in this group. It's so striking to see work of women writers figuring so prominently on the scene. The people you should be aware of are Shahrnush Parsipur and Moniru Ravanipur, both [of whom] write in enchanting Iranian varieties of magical realism; Goli Taraghi, a magnificent storyteller who depicts some of the most tragic situations in contemporary Iran with wit and humor; Zoya Pirzad, a highly talented writer whose stories and novels capture a very complex and interesting picture of the sociology of contemporary Iran, particularly the situation of women; Ghazaleh Alizadeh, a great writer, who unfortunately passed away; [and] Farkhondeh

Hajizadeh, Farkhondeh Aghai, Fereshteh Sari, Tahereh Alavi, Shiva Arastui, Sepideh Shamlu, Soudabeh Ashrafi, Fereshteh Molavi, and many more. These women are breaking the molds and are experimenting with new genres and styles of writing.

Some of the remarkable male writers who have gained fame after the revolution are Javad Mojabi, Amir Hosein Cheheltan, Jafar Modares Sadeghi, Shahriyar Mandanipour, Nassim Khaksar, Bijan Najdi, Abutorab Khosravi, Hassan Sanapour, Reza Farokhfal, Reza Daneshvar, and Ghazi Rabihavi. Both men and women—I separated them only because I wanted to stress the importance of a large number of women entering the literary scene— write in styles that have been characterized as magical realist, neorealist, and postmodern.

Because of the contemporary move away from social realism of the 1960s and 1970s, and also because of the practice of censorship, you see people beginning to tell personal stories based on real lives; but these personal stories are also political. In postrevolutionary Iranian literature, you see an intersection between the personal and political in a way you did not see before the revolution. Before the revolution the literature was very influenced by political grand narratives and was at times somewhat didactic. After the revolution you see the same kind of political awareness, but placed in more interesting personal situations. Writers have become more introspective in the choice of their subjects and themes. Aspects of Iranian history, culture, and tradition are explored and dissected, perhaps to arrive at a critique of the present by seeking clues in the past or in the culture or religion. You also see the emergence of new genres and a lot of experimentation with different styles. The sheer volume of literary production exploded after the revolution and particularly after the war. It was no longer confined to the realm of a small, educated, elite group of writers and poets from the major cities. In contemporary Iran, I think writing has moved from the private space of an elite group of writers and readers to the public space.

By the way, much of what I have said refers to writers and poets writing in Persian in exile as well as those writing in Iran. Writers and poets in exile have been tremendously productive. In the work of the first generation after the revolution, we witness a certain level of nostalgia, but also attempts to seek new ways of expression unconcerned with the kind of censorship they had to worry about at home.

So far, I have only spoken about prose, but much of what I said about the use of new genres and experimentation applies to contemporary poetry, as well. The poetry editor for *Strange Times* is Dr. Ahmad Karimi Hakkak. As he and other literary critics point out, contemporary poetry is also less obviously political; it is introspective, image-centered, and relevant at the same time. Poets invoke new interpretations of the past, play with memory, and experiment with new meanings for traditional symbols. Given the rich classical poetic tradition in our culture, there is a fiery debate going on among poets about what constitutes "real" poetry. Many of those trained in the classical tradition reject some of the abstract postmodern styles and experimentation with meaning that younger poets engage in.

One of the most important facts to note about writers and poets in Iran is that they actually cannot make their living as writers. Most of the people, who have been producing some excellent novels, stories, and poems, have two or three other jobs. They also have to go through the rigorous censorship system, which was a bit relaxed during the presidency of Mohammad Khatami (1997–2005) but is being tightened again since Mahmoud Ahmadinejad was elected president in June 2005. So I think you really have to be committed to be a writer or a poet in Iran, since it doesn't pay financially, you're often in trouble with one or the other branch of the regime, and you have to go through a complex bureaucracy of censorship.

When I was there, I was trying to find out what a writer has to do from the minute he or she finishes a manuscript to the moment that it comes out in bookstores. There are about seven difficult stages that they have to go through, and a publishing permit can be rejected at each point. Books are sometimes banned after one week on the shelf of the bookstore, incurring financial losses for publishers as well as writers. So it requires remarkable dedication to be a writer or a publisher in Iran.

Speaking of censorship, Abbas Kiarostami, a leading filmmaker, said that he had difficulty including a couplet from the classic Iranian poet Omar Khayyám in one of his films.

Sometimes you can't even try to figure out why. It's partly luck. It depends on who you get as your censor. Some censors are more intelligent, or more liberal, or more reformist. When you look in the bookstores in Iran, you see quite a variety of books on many different subjects. And occasionally, parts of books that are published and available make you wonder how they possibly got through. Aside from the overall prohibitions on insulting Islam, the clergy, or the leaders, some censors are more sensitive to political matters, and others are strictly religious and are looking for sexual connotations to cross out.

I was speaking to a writer—his name is Ghazi Rabihavi—who has a very interesting story which he published in the magazine *Index on Censorship*. Describing himself he says:

> Once upon a time an Iranian writer wrote a 179-page-long novel. And, like every other Iranian writer, he presented it to the Ministry of Islamic Guidance to receive a publication permit. Then the writer waited. His book began with the following passage. "She knew that once her husband had

brought her a cup of coffee, she would feel better, like every other day. As she stood by the window, the wind slid gently over her brown arms, and her eyes were on the rising sun that was pulling itself up over the government buildings. It was a sunrise that was like a sunset." After 13 months spent climbing up the slippery ladder of bureaucracy, the Iranian writer finally managed to obtain an appointment with the director in charge of censorship. The director was just a head. His body was hidden behind the desk and it seemed to be reclining gently against something soft. The head delivered the following speech to the writer. "Unfortunately, your book has some small problems which cannot be corrected. I'm certain you will agree with me. Take these first few sentences. Nowhere in our noble culture will you find any woman who would allow herself to stand waiting for her husband to bring her a cup of coffee, okay? Well, the next problem is the image of the wind sliding over the naked arms, which is provocative and has sexual overtones.

Finally, nowhere in any noble culture will you find a sunrise that is like a sunset. Maybe it's a misprint. Here you are, then. Here's your book. I hope you will write another book soon. We support you, we support you." And the head slid back under the desk.

This quote gives you an idea of how a few sentences can be interpreted by one censor. In fact, many Iranian writers have had manuscripts rejected by the censor and had to wait a year or so for another chance to submit them so that perhaps another censor would look through them and maybe they would get through.

Kiarostami also recounts that when he made a film called The Wind Will Carry Us, *which is still banned, incidentally, he had a couple of verses by Forugh Farrokhzad. Who is she, and why is she important?*

She is one of the finest female poets we have had in the modern period. She unfortunately died in a car accident in 1967 at the age of thirty-two. Her work is essentially feminist. In her poetry, she gives women a voice in terms of sensuality and desire, as well as in terms of intellectual aspiration in poetry, philosophy, and art. She was a modern woman. She was divorced, had relationships with men, and lived a very full intellectual and artistic life. So I think that for the Islamist regime she's the symbol of the "wayward" woman, a model that they think nobody else in the Islamic Republic should aspire to. Some of her work cannot be published, and she's regarded as very threatening to the way they would like to depict women.

Talk about the oral tradition in Iran. Perhaps you cannot find a book of poetry by Farrokhzad but people know her couplets and poems, and recite them.

I was talking with my nephew. He's in his twenties and was brought up in the West. He went to Iran and spent the summer of 2006 working there. He was saying when he went to parties or talked to young people his own age, he was impressed with many things, including the number of poems that they could recite by heart. This is part of Iranian tradition, and it's also entrenched in the educational system. We had to memorize two or three poems a month in our Persian literature classes. Some of them were quite long. Also, poetry crosses class lines. Because people are familiar with poetry through education and the oral tradition, it is read out loud on special occasions, memorized, recited, and used as points of reference in daily lives. Poetry is often cited in proverbs. So, yes, this oral and poetic tradition is extremely vibrant in Iran. Even political slogans often rhyme, and we have a strong tradition of satirical poetry.

Is there any kind of samizdat movement as in the Soviet Union, where underground press publications and newsletters circulated?

The situation in Iran is different from that of the old Soviet Union in several important ways. In the Soviet Union, the state and the party had a unified policy against dissidents and intellectuals, who, in turn, were pretty united amongst themselves, at least in terms of their short-term goals for freedom of thought and expression. In the Iranian case, there were divisions and differing perspectives within both the state and the opposition such that we did not develop a samizdat-like underground press and communication system. We now have more of a samizdat-like movement among the bloggers on the Internet, and I will talk about them later. Let me explain about the writers and intellectuals first.

After the war with Iraq, which ended in 1988, Rafsanjani came to power, portraying himself as a pragmatic Islamist. When he was president, there was some relaxing of the total power of ideology on everyday aspects of life. He wasn't interested in democracy, but in opening up the markets. In fact, during his presidency, a lot of intellectuals who were active in trying to organize a writers' organization were targeted, killed, and otherwise silenced. He wanted to loosen the strings a little in terms of everyday life so that people could breathe and so that business would flourish. What ensued was that the people began to demand a freer press, more variety of newspapers, more public discussion.

And then we have Khatami, who was elected as president rather unexpectedly in 1997. He was elected because of his promises, not only of establishing a more open society where people wouldn't be constantly afraid of the vice squads harassing women and young people, or of religious police bursting into houses and finding a bottle of wine or a pack of cards, but the promise that the laws would be changed to make basic citizens' rights more permanent and not totally dependent on the whim of who happens to be in power.

Khatami wanted to put a kinder, gentler face on the Islamic Republic by concentrating on more freedom in civil society, a more relaxed implementation of Islamist laws, more dialogue among different groups in society. People, particularly women and youth, voted for him overwhelmingly. And for a few years there was some opening, the reformist press began to thrive, and there was even some space for secular intellectuals in publications relating to philosophy, culture, and the arts. As one blogger referring to the Khatami years puts it, "We got concerts, poetry readings, carefree chats in coffee shops, and tight *manteaus* [the tunics women are required to wear]. But is this all my generation wanted?"

However, Khatami was just one part of the leadership. There were lots of organizations and leaders within the Islamic regime, such as the judiciary and the security forces, who were against this kind of opening. They saw it as a weakening of the foundation of Islamist rule. Consequently, there were many crackdowns on newspapers, journalists, writers, and artists. The internal power struggle, between the different factions of the Islamic Republic, and the harshness with which the conservative institutions, such as the judiciary, treated dissidents, *and* the lack of unity between dissidents created a special situation whereby there was some discussion and dialogue at the intellectual level, but this dialogue did not translate into concrete changes in law or state policies toward people who strayed from the accepted ideology. Secular intellectuals and dissidents benefited from the openings but did not join the reformist movement or trust it because of its essentially Islamist agenda. In the end, most reformists were stifled, as well.

The problem with intellectuals, writers, and artists in Iran—and this goes back over a hundred years—is that they do not have an independent support base. A lot of them, as I said, do not make their living from their profession. Many of them are bureaucrats, or teachers, and thus dependent on the state for their survival. They can't afford to continually challenge the government. Many of them have bravely done so; some have lost their lives. But in order for a genuine resistance movement to take root, you need organization, which intellectuals and artists often lack. In fact, there isn't consensus among them about precise political goals. While they agree that they don't want an Islamic state or another form of dictatorship, there is a lively debate and discussion about the shape of a future state. This is an Iranian debate—in reaching a consensus, they certainly don't want to turn to the outside world, since support from the outside is never quite disinterested. Historically, Iran has not had a good experience with outsiders trying to control what direction our politics and society should take. We were in a semicolonial situation, manipulated by Britain and Russia throughout the nineteenth century, and then in the twentieth century we were stuck in middle of the struggle between the Soviet Union and the United States. Several democratic movements in Iran—the constitutional revolution of 1906–11 and the democratic government of Prime Minister Mossadegh in 1951–53, were either undermined or overthrown directly by outside intervention.

There really isn't such an independent international community today as there was then. The reality now is that whoever tries to help a movement for democracy is doing so for their own self-interest. I think the people in the Middle East have very little faith in westerners trying to bring them democracy at this point. They have a historical memory and know that western regimes, more often than not, have backed dictators, and have undermined and overthrown budding democratic movements. So the intellectuals are sensitive to this. Let me give you an example.

Akbar Ganji recently came to the West. He is the journalist who was imprisoned for years because of his participation in the Berlin conference in 2000, where some of the reformist intellectuals and writers had come to discuss parliamentary democracy in Iran. Upon their return, the conservative judiciary had them all arrested. Akbar Ganji had been an Islamist, a member of Revolutionary Guard, and a very committed follower of Khomeini. But he changed over the years and had come to the conclusion that a theocratic state was not going to work, that Islam is a very respectable religion but that it had to be separated from politics, and that the rule of the clerics was antidemocratic by nature. He wrote about all these things in his articles. And he was arrested, and throughout the six years that he was imprisoned, he resisted, went on many hunger strikes, and never gave up his principles.

In the West, Ganji won praise and awards for his bravery in prison and for continuing to write about democracy in Iran. Wherever he was traveling and speaking, he made sure that every speech he made contained the declaration that he was not going to be accepting any money from any western government, that he was not going to be meeting officially with any government officials, especially those from the Bush administration in the United States.

Independence is a very important condition for the success of any democratic and progressive movement in Iran, because there is continuous suspicion that westerners are trying to influence events. The regime in Iran exploits this to the fullest, because when someone makes a comment that they don't like or when dissidents or secularists speak, they are often accused of working for foreign interests. They are accused of receiving money or support from international organizations or outside institutions. The regime is genuinely worried about the "velvet revolution" phenomenon, and they use the pretext to discredit internal dissidents this way. So it's a very sensitive issue with intellectuals and writers.

In 2003, Zahra Kazemi, an Iranian-born Canadian journalist, died while in state custody. Talk about her case and its significance.

Zahra Kazemi's death occurred at a time of intense competition between the conservative judiciary and intelligence agency and the reformist parliament and president. She was arrested on June 23, 2003, as she took photographs of the family members of detained students demonstrating in front of Evin Prison. She died nineteen days later, after being severely beaten in custody. Initially, the government insisted her death was accidental. After an outcry from the reformists and the Canadian government, Khatami ordered an investigation. But the multiple investigations and the trial that ensued only reflected the overriding power of the conservatives in the judiciary and the powerlessness of the ministers in Khatami's government and the reformist parliamentarians. It sounds Orwellian, but Saeed Mortazavi, the prosecutor general who had closed down scores of reformist newspapers and who had been complicit in the torture and murder of many prisoners, including Zahra Kazemi, was appointed to lead an investigation into the causes of her death!

Subsequently, two intelligence agents who had interrogated her were charged with her death, and Shirin Ebadi represented the Kazemi family at the trial. None of the defense requests for witnesses were granted, and eventually the agents were acquitted by the judge. The trial was a sham.

In my opinion, the conservatives made an example of Zahra Kazemi for two main reasons. First, to show the reformists that they commanded power over the vital organs of government. Second, to dissuade journalists and human-rights advocates from investigating the activities of the intelligence ministry and the judiciary, particularly with respect to the treatment of prisoners. Obviously what happened to Zahra Kazemi does not bode well for journalists or for Iranians abroad who return home for visits. It shocked and frightened people and probably caused many to steer clear of politics when they return.

It's interesting to compare Mohammad Khatami, who was a cleric, elected twice as president, to Mahmoud Ahmadinejad, the current president. He was the former mayor of Tehran, obviously not a cleric, but seems to espouse more Islamist views than Mohammad Khatami.

Ahmadinejad is quite an interesting phenomenon. I think he represents the nonclerical conservative faction. There is a sense among more educated middle-class Iranians that a creeping coup d'état by nonclerical conservative Islamists connected to the Revolutionary Guard and *baseej* paramilitary forces is occurring. The Guard and *baseej* formations were involved in the Iran–Iraq war as young men, and today many of them are in positions of power. These forces constitute Ahmadinejad's core constituency. They feel that they can be the new face of conservative Islam in a more economically just and efficient way than the clerics were. They address the gap between the rich and the poor and the corruption among powerful clerics and their cronies, who have enriched themselves.

Khatami, on the other hand, is an unusual cleric. He's highly educated, and I think he deeply believes in the things that he says—about the dialogue of civilizations, the importance of the rule of law, the blending of the positive aspects of Islam with the positive aspects of the West, the maintenance of cultural authenticity for Iran. But he was more of an academic or a diplomat than politician. And I don't think that he was willing to stick his neck out to create any major turmoil to stand up for his beliefs.

But ultimately in the political structure the rahbar, the leader, has ultimate power, and that is Ayatollah Ali Khamenei.

Yes. If you look at the power structure of the state, it's extremely difficult for any president to undermine the Council of Guardians, the Council of Expediency, the judiciary, the Revolutionary Guard, the *baseej*, the powerful foundations, and, of course, the *rahbar*, or supreme leader. The clerics that are still part of the old Islamist establishment that came to power after the revolution would like to maintain their domination of the army, the judiciary, all the militias, and the powerful, wealthy foundations. It's extremely difficult to challenge this kind of power structure, in which clerical power has been constitutionally and legally locked in.

But it's not impossible. Various dissident groups have different ways of looking at how change is possible in Iran. Discontent is pervasive among the youth, women, workers, professionals, students, and ethnic and tribal groups. But it hasn't been articulated in a unified, organized movement. Every once in a while, expressions of discontent break out. In 2006, workers from the bus transportation union went on strike. Their leaders have been jailed and their families punished. The principal leader, Mohammad Reza Ossanlou, was subsequently released, but due to its independence, the union is heavily monitored by the regime.

Teachers and university professors are periodically targeted. In late 2006, many secular and reformist professors were forcibly "retired" or simply fired, after Ahmadinejad made clear that the regime should eradicate the influence of secular education from high school and university curricula. Liberal Islamists (*Nehzat-e Azadi*), reformists of various kinds who have broken from the regime, secular social democrats, socialists, youth, many women's groups—all can be considered as dissidents in search of ways to organize and unite. Many say that resistance can be successful only through mobilizing the population to support the separation of state and religion through peaceful means and civil disobedience. They believe that civil disobedience has worked successfully against formidably powerful foes without too much violence in other historical instances, and it can work in Iran. Some say that changes should be attempted through elections, through repeated efforts to get more reformists into parliament, in the presidency, and in the other bodies that run the Islamic Republic, and to change things gradually that way.

One of the largest dissident groups in Iran is a cluster of student organizations who believe in change through grassroots organizing, demonstrations, civil disobedience, and direct participation in elections. The student movement showed itself to be threatening enough to be crushed by the government in 1999. There were major student demonstrations in that year; several students were killed and many were imprisoned. One of them, Akbar Mohammadi, died recently in prison. His family complained that he had been tortured and beaten, and he had been on a hunger strike, as well. Though the regime has reacted very harshly against the students, they are resilient and patient. They express their discontent whenever and wherever possible.

I would say that many of the dissidents loosely fit into the category we can call republicans, not in the current American sense, but people who want a new constitution for a secular, democratic state, the freedom to establish political parties, free elections, social justice. They don't want to go back to the monarchy, and thus the term *republican*. But they obviously want a secular state. They're not an organized group but a loose coalition of people with support among educated professionals, the middle class, and the lower middle class. As far as I know, none of these groups believes in a violent overthrow of the regime.

This has very distinct historical reasons. I was talking to a member of the student movement. He was saying, "Look, every time we had a violent overthrow of a regime, we had more bloodshed. Violence breeds violence." His comments reflect a widespread sense of fatigue with revolution and war. People want to settle down and lead normal lives. Even though they can disagree with their government, and they suffer under it, opting for revolution without a clear vision of the future is not something that any of the groups, except some of the fringe ones, might want to do.

Another point that almost all dissident groups share is that they do not want interference by the United States, or by any other power, in the affairs of

Iran. Presently, the U.S. is the power most inclined to threaten invasion or interference in Iran. The U.S. is occupying Iran's neighbors, Afghanistan and Iraq. U.S. naval armadas control the seas. U.S. satellites and air force control the skies. The U.S. has bases all over the Middle East. All of the dissidents agree that outside interference or manipulation would be disastrous, with the exception of some dissident groups outside Iran, like the monarchists and the *mojaheddin-e khalq*. The latter would like to see American muscle overthrow the Islamic Republic and thereby have a chance to take power for themselves.

And obviously the monarchists want the restoration of the Pahlavi Dynasty? Where are they based?

They are concentrated in the Washington, D.C., area, where the son of the former shah and some of the older generals and the monarchist loyalists reside. They are also in the Los Angeles area, where there is the largest community of Iranians. I think the U.S. Congress has given the monarchists substantial financial support. They have a television station based in Los Angeles that broadcasts to Iran. The programming consists of music, soap operas, and stories about celebrities, as well as pro-monarchist news and ideology. My impression is that the people in Iran sometimes watch these programs for their entertainment value but they don't take them very seriously from a political point of view.

Who are the oppositional figures active in Iran that you think people should know about? You mentioned Akbar Ganji.

Akbar Ganji is a very smart, interesting, and brave man. However, I see him as an example of a reformed Islamist who has relatively recently discovered the benefits of the separation of religion and state. It's very interesting—he actually peppers his speeches with quotes from Hegel, Kant, and even John Rawls. He says Iran needs to change, that Iranians need to have a secular state with a free parliamentary system. He focuses on equal rights for men and women, and he focuses on human rights as a very important aspect of any future Iranian government. He also talks about how we have to establish truth and reconciliation committees instead of using violence to resolve past injustices, how we have to abolish the death penalty, and how, under whatever government we adopt in the future, we shouldn't repeat the cycle of death and revenge that we've had before. What he says sounds very reasonable.

My problem with it is that he sounds like this is the first time anyone is making such proposals in Iran. And that's simply not the case. There were progressive, leftist, social democratic, and democratic movements in various other times in Iranian history, and since the revolution, that have made similar proposals. I'm happy to say that after the tough experiences of the revolution, of war, and of the Islamic Republic, many people who are seeking democracy in Iran are putting their finger on the problem of violence in our politics and are saying, "No, violence is not the answer."

I don't want to overemphasize the importance of Ganji—he is one among many. A number of experienced and politically savvy people in Iran are not openly active in politics, as they have been imprisoned or banned from teaching and public speaking. They are soaking in the lessons of our recent history and looking for innovative strategies of resistance and desirable future forms of government. A prime example is Abbas Amir-Entezam, who has been in prison for twenty-six years. Rather than seeking this or that public personality as an answer to our political dilemma, I observe evidence of the silent majority waiting for an opportunity to express itself and of various groups in society attempting to find peaceful, long-term road maps for change.

For example, I hugely respect groups of activists—journalists, lawyers, academics, poets, writers, doctors—who are battling the political and social problems steadfastly, stubbornly, patiently, against all odds. Shirin Ebadi, and her activities in defense of women's rights, children's rights, and the rights of political prisoners, is the obvious example. Simin Behbahani, the brilliant contemporary poet, is a prime example of political courage and resilience to her admirers. Nasser Zarafshan is a courageous lawyer who often defends writers and intellectuals and is now in Evin Prison for doing his job. But there are lots of others—many of them women—who are trying to change things gradually through their participation in the NGOs [nongovernmental organizations], in civil society, and within their professions, to challenge divorce laws, custody rights, even things like insurance for single women. They are working gradually to institute a ban on polygamy, to institute equal rights to divorce, to institute laws for joint custody, to abolish stoning as punishment, and to raise the minimum age of marriage for girls. Initially the minimum age of marriage for girls was *nine years*. Through the efforts of brave individuals and women's groups, they moved it to fifteen, and now they're trying to move it to eighteen.

So there is so much going on at the grassroots level. These are the people I respect most, the activists who work in many of the NGOs and charities, working to battle the terrible drug problem among the youth, working on environmental issues. Iran has one of the worst cases of pollution in the world. Tehran is just as bad as Mexico City, if not worse. There are lots of groups working with issues like earthquake and disaster relief, domestic abuse, runaway girls, and homeless kids. The NGOs have evolved as sites where secular people can be involved in their society without being overtly political and thereby getting into trouble. These activists are working gradually to increase awareness, to organize others, to try to motivate the youth.

Is it relatively easy for a woman to get a divorce in Iran?

It's much easier for a man. The man can basically get a divorce if and when he wants. A woman can file for a divorce if she has permission from her husband(!) or if she can prove that her husband is insane, addicted, or impotent. Domestic abuse is increasingly being taken seriously as a just cause for divorce. A woman has to go before an Islamic judge and try to argue her case, with or without the help of a lawyer. One of the most difficult aspects of applications for divorce is the question of child custody, which customarily goes to the man after the age of seven. But the laws are being challenged by women all the time.

What about property rights?

Women can own, buy, or sell property. The inequalities in the law are most blatant in terms of divorce, inheritance, child custody, reproductive rights, and travel restrictions—a women needs her husband's permission to travel abroad. The situation in Iran is very complex, though. Maybe some background will clarify what I mean.

Women were very active in the opposition movements against the shah and in the revolution itself.

With the victory of the Islamist forces, in the first years of the revolution, the ideal image of the "Muslim woman" was the main basis of state legislation and policy toward women. This meant the *sharia,* or the body of Islamic law as interpreted by the Shia clergy, was reimposed as the main basis of the law of the land. (By the way, the *sharia* had always been used in the regulation of marriage, divorce, custody, etc., even at the time of the shah, but some changes had occurred that had modified the *sharia* and were beneficial to women, including the Family Protection Law of the 1970s.) This meant the exclusion of women from certain professions—judgeships, for example (Shirin Ebadi lost her job)—the imposition of the Islamic dress code, and strict *sharia* rules in the regulation of life, including divorce, inheritance, child custody, and reproductive rights. Strict sharia punishments were also imposed, such as stoning for adultery (for both men and women). However, women could still vote and still participate in the political process, short of attaining high office.

Then, in this complex situation, where women were, at the same time, politically present yet socially and legally excluded, the Iran–Iraq war occurred. The war, as historically wars have done in many societies, mobilized women to become involved in the economy and in the public sphere. So now, the regime's propaganda that good Muslim women should stay at home and take care of the kids became irrelevant; their skills were needed to maintain the economy in wartime. Large numbers of women began to work in government offices, banks, health care, and in various other tasks behind the front, enhancing their economic position in society. Unexpectedly, the war contributed to certain legal changes that were beneficial to women, as well. For example, when a husband was killed in the war, according to Islamic law, the custody of the children (and veteran benefits) would immediately transfer to the husband's family, leaving the wife without husband, child, or income. After many complaints by the wives of the soldiers killed in the war, the parliament finally passed a law in 1985 allowing mothers to keep the children and to collect government benefits.

After the war with Iraq ended in 1988, women were needed more than ever to help in the reconstruction of the country. Women became more officially accepted in many of the professions they had been discouraged from entering, including law, medicine, and many technical areas. This economic reintegration had its political consequences—more women candidates ran for office, and were elected, not only in Tehran, but in the provinces, as well. Several women even tried to run for president but were struck down by the Council of Guardians. In the fifth and sixth parliaments, that is, between 1996 and 2005, various attempts were made by women and men parliamentarians of the reformist movement to change the laws regarding divorce, rape, and marriage age. Now, over 60 percent of university students are women, and women graduates are more numerous than men. Many are no longer in traditional women's fields like education and nursing and are engineers, scientists, physicists, and physicians. So the consequences of these trends will continue to be felt in the economy and will put pressure on the regime to change the laws.

In short, the legal situation of women has been difficult but not static; it has been evolving in the public and private spheres. And throughout these years, women have taken their specific grievances to the courts, asking for reinterpretations of the sharia to redress the injustices; consequently, the courts and the legal domain have become the central focus for women in their demands for change.

Is there a women's movement in Iran?

Women began their formal struggle for legal equality around the time of the Iranian constitutional revolution one hundred years ago. And with various advances, ups and downs, steps forward and backward, this struggle continues today. Presently, the women's movement consists of a loose coalition of organizations and individuals. The composition of the movement that has evolved from all these complex experiences that I mentioned is quite diverse. There are women who believe in an Islamic form of government but believe in a different, flexible, more woman-friendly interpretation of Islamic law. There are those who are believers from a religious background but desire the separation of religion from politics and the secularization of the legal system. And of course, there are various configurations of secular women. All fight the laws gradually through the legal system and defy the laws when they can. More recently, they have been holding open demonstrations with specific demands. The majority are professionals, students, and middle class. Young or old, pious or secular, they frame their demands in legal terms and basic women's-rights terms. They want a ban on polygamy, equal rights to divorce for men and women, joint custody or the possibility of sole woman's custody, equal rights in marriage. In addition, they want the minimum age for marriage increased. They want the lifting of the remaining restrictions on their professional choices and on attaining high political office.

I mentioned that women have been recently holding open demonstrations. It is important to mention that for the last two years, there have been demonstrations and sit-ins to protest the injustices to women in the Iranian constitution. Article 20 of the Iranian constitution states that men and women "enjoy equal protection of the law . . . in conformity with Islamic criteria," and Article 21 ensures the rights of women, again "in conformity with Islamic criteria." The women argue that effectively, "Islamic criteria" or their interpretation have resulted in unjust laws for women and that therefore the constitution must be changed. The organization and publicity around these demonstrations shows the existence of a large coalition of groups and individuals from all over the country, including men. Despite a great deal of internal and international support, a demonstration in 2006 was brutally disrupted just as the participants were assembling. A new all-woman police force attacked and beat the demonstrators with batons as the policemen looked on. Seventy women and men were arrested. Even before the demonstration, a number of women's-rights and human-rights activists were summoned before the courts. But this was the first time we've seen the conservatives train a highly accomplished *female* police force to attack women.

Why is that?

Since the election of Ahmadinejad, there have been rumblings of crackdowns on personal and political freedoms. The Islamist conservatives regard developments in civil society as threatening and susceptible to foreign manipulation. Various conservatives have been talking publicly about this—even the conservative paper *Jomhuri Eslami* stated that most of the NGOs are run by secularists and reformists, and that women's NGOs are acting as agents of the West. They actually point to the collapse of the Soviet Union as a direct result of the expansion of civil society, and they call the NGOs and other cultural organizations entities that are not in line with Islamist thinking.

I think the general trend with Ahmadinejad has been to try to Islamicize civil society wherever he can. In other words, to create Islamist NGOs and to choke the other NGOs out. When he presented his budget to the parliament, there was very limited funding for NGOs. Most of them are independent anyway. But some that were involved in charities did receive some help from the government, which he cut. Instead, he gave more money to the mosques and Islamic organizations. So they want to crack down on non-Islamist groups by force—female or male police, the *baseej*, the Revolutionary Guard, the vigilante groups—by choking them financially, or by Islamicizing them. They've been trying all three approaches on various NGOs.

What about reproductive rights?

Abortion is illegal, and contraception was initially discouraged, as Iranians were told to go forth and multiply by Ayatollah Khomeini. But with the subsequent population explosion and the ensuing economic problems, the state changed its policies with respect to contraception, which is now readily available and distributed in state clinics and hospitals.

These women's groups, do they take the form of NGOs?

They take the form of NGOs, as well as Web sites, magazines, journals, cultural and educational associations, artists' groups, student organizations, professional organizations—for example, there is an association of women publishers. There are women bloggers. A number of the bloggers who have been arrested in the last year have been women. And there are various feminist Web sites that are interesting to look at. Through this network of formal and informal communications, the women organize demonstrations and letter-writing campaigns and engage in lobbying and pressuring government officials.

The interesting thing that I found out during the summer of 2006 was that there seems to be quite a large number of women who get elected and become active in small-scale politics like neighborhood councils, city councils, and school boards.

They organize very well, and they set specific goals and they achieve them. It's amazing how they have been able to achieve small victories and represent and promote their points of view.

Talk about women and Islam and the issue of dress.

There is a lot happening underneath the surface. The *hejab,* or Islamic cover, is all about interpretation. In the Koran and other sources of the *sharia,* the requirement is that women be dressed with modesty. Historically, each Muslim community has interpreted this injunction differently and according to their own local traditions. As the revolution was occurring in Iran, some women put on scarves as a sign of their association with the Islamist cause, some as a symbol of resistance to the shah, and many women didn't wear any cover at all. Then Khomeini made the question of *hejab* a legal issue after the revolution. At that time, nobody thought that Islamic cover was going to be imposed by law, and there was quite a bit of resistance to it. But they made it a legal matter in the first stage of the revolution, when the Islamist identity of the revolution was a major priority for those who came to power.

Historically, the control of women's appearance, bodies, skills, and place in society seems to be symbolically important for every new regime that assumes power. Once Islamic cover was legislated, with the different stages of the Islamist rule came different levels of compliance and enforcement. Now women show the spectrum of political/cultural feelings about the regime by the way they wear their *hejab*—of course, within the framework of acceptable styles that doesn't get them arrested.

How much hair could you show, if any?

It varies how much hair you could show, or how long your *manteau* or tunic can be. Technically, thighs have to be covered, below the knee. In times of tougher enforcement, the tunic had to be well below the knee, and you could not show your feet, you couldn't show nails with nail polish, you couldn't wear sandals. You had to wear long pants or thick stockings, as well. No flesh was supposed to show except for the face. And in the early part of the revolution—some of these are rumors, by the way—but people were saying if you have beautiful eyes, you have to wear glasses because beautiful eyes would attract men. That never became law, but you would see some of the very religious women with gloves and dark glasses so you couldn't see their eyes.

For government workers, bureaucrats, and teachers, there is a uniform head scarf, *maghnaeh,* and it covers part of the forehead and it comes up to the chin and falls so that only the round part of your face is showing. That is actually easier, because it's like a uniform, and you don't have to worry about whether something that's not supposed to be showing becomes exposed, although it's quite uncomfortable. So working women, like, nurses, bureaucrats, teachers, all of them have to wear that in their place of work. It's when you're going shopping or going out to the restaurant that you can play around with what kind of *hejab* you wear. You have the whole spectrum among women in Iran today. There are fully covered women, and then there are women with tight jeans, a tight tunic above the knees, high heels, makeup, and a small scarf on their head with lots of hair showing.

What's the difference between hejab *and* chador?

Hejab means "cover," basically, so it could come in many different forms. *Chador* is just one of the forms. That's the loose, long, traditional piece of cloth that some Iranian women wear. You don't see those in Arab countries, certainly not in Afghanistan, because their *hejab* is much more substantial.

There it's the burqa.

The *chador* is a loose, long piece of cloth. It's open in the front, and you can wrap it around when you need to, and unwrap it and move your hands freely when not in the presence of men who are strangers. And some *chadors*—I remember my grandmother had some party *chadors* that were like see-through lace, beautiful, hand-embroidered. It wasn't really covering anything. It was a part of a woman's clothes, traditionally.

Are there any legal challenges to these dress codes?

This is interesting. When I was looking at the demands of the most radical students in the universities who want a secular state, their demands included equality of rights between men and women, but none of them mention the *hejab*. And this is because they think that contesting the *hejab* is a divisive factor. If you argue with them, they say that they're afraid that the conservatives will pick on them if they openly advocate the removal of *hejab*, because that could be used as the loosening-of-women paradigm. That is to say, all who want political and legal change will be framed as people who want to abuse your daughters, who want to open up society to corruption and take Iran back to the old miniskirt days of the shah's time. So everyone who is advocating for change *within Iran* has not yet touched the *hejab* issue. The women don't refer to it openly in their demands, but I think it is definitely implied in the other legal demands.

Do you think it's an important issue?

Very much so. In fact, I had a debate with a student about this. I said, "When you're advocating the legal equality of men and women, how can you *not* specifically address the issue of freedom of clothing? How can you not resist the law that *hejab* is compulsory?" He said, "Our position on the legal equality of men and women includes the freedom of choice for clothing. It's implicit that *hejab* would not be compulsory. But we don't want to give this weapon to the conservatives." He said that the majority of people in Iran are not fanatics but they are believers, especially when you get out of the cities and go into the smaller towns and the countryside. I think this is true: to them, there is a sense of tradition involved in the *hejab*. And if it is to be changed, it has to be changed gradually, and without the interference of the government.

I was in France in 2005–6 and was involved in some debates about *l'affaire du voile*—"the affair of the veil." They have a law that you cannot wear Islamic cover in public schools or government buildings. If you're a Muslim girl and want to go to a public school, within the parameters of the school you have to take off your veil. They based this law on the argument of *laïcité*—secularism—as a fundamental principle of the French state. In other words, manifesting difference of religion by wearing a headscarf or a big cross or a yarmulke—creates differences among the students and could lead to discrimination. Anything that ostensibly shows your religion is prohibited.

We were having discussions about this, and I was saying that in my opinion the state should have nothing to do with what people wear or not wear, because once you legislate clothing, then it could go either way. And Iran is the best example. Reza Shah, the father of Mohammad Reza Shah, who was overthrown in 1979, criminalized the veil, so you had soldiers taking off veils from women's heads by force in the 1930s. It created a lot of discomfort and cultural confusion. Reza Shah believed that in order for Iran to become modern, women had to look more like western women, so while women could not wear veils, they could wear western-style hats. There are many photographs of women from that period, many looking awkward and uncomfortable, with traditional long dresses and western hats propped up on their heads. They look like strange products of a social-engineering experiment. Apparently, some women totally refused to go outdoors without their scarves or *chadors*.

Then gradually, within two or three generations, people got used to not wearing the veil. Also, Mohammad Reza Shah relaxed that law, so by the 1950s women could wear their preferred form of *hejab* if they wished or go without head cover altogether. Then during this regime it was legislated that women have to wear (certain state/clergy-endorsed forms of) *hejab*. There has been and is a lot of resistance to that, as well. In my opinion, the dissidents haven't brought this up because it's a very divisive issue; in a sense it will have to follow other, more fundamental changes such as the separation of religion and state in Iran. I'm sure that as we advance toward a more secular state, the women's groups will make this demand. We're not there yet.

You mentioned bloggers encountering difficulties with the state. Is Internet use widespread in the country?

I think Persian is the fourth-most-prominent blogger language in the world. This community of bloggers grew over a relatively short period of time. The story is that an Iranian journalist, Hossein Derakhshan, moved to Canada and wrote an easy guide to blogging in Persian. Thousands began to write on blogs, and the number grew every day, because for a while, it was a safe way to express opinions from the personal to the political in a society where self-expression is highly dangerous. There's a fine book on the topic, *We Are Iran,* by Nasrin Alavi. She has compiled a collection from the writing of the 64,000 or so bloggers writing in Persian. The bloggers write about everything—from the difficulties of growing up as a young person in Iran, to problems of love, marriage, drugs, *hejab*, prejudice, patriarchy in its various forms, cinema, art, politics, elections, natural disasters, human rights. The blogs present an interesting portrait of the energy, the promise, the contradictions and tragedies of contemporary Iran.

The government first clamped down on the bloggers in 2003, when they arrested a journalist, Sina Motallebi, who wrote for a popular weblog. That was just the beginning; many others were subsequently arrested, including women, imprisoned, and forced into sordid confessions. As a result of this policy toward the Internet and blogging, a lot of bloggers have gone underground.

I was told by one young person that when Iranian technicians and young mathematicians—they're smart and often get prizes in international competitions—are censored, they figure out ways to bypass government controls to access the Web.

It's like the reformist press movement of the 1990s. If one newspaper got a little too daring in its critique and was closed down, a few journalists or the editor would go to jail for a few months. Then they would come out and the editor's uncle or brother-in-law would apply for another permit, and they would start another newspaper under another name. There were so many newspapers that went through different life cycles that way. Iranians are very persistent.

The Internet is not only an important source of information for Iranians, but also a source of entertainment and a way to connect to the outside world. The youth are educated and energetic. There is high unemployment and a limited number of entertainment choices. During the Khatami period, Iranian rock bands were given permits to perform, and concerts attracted thousands of spectators. But since Ahmadinejad was elected, no band received a permit to give a concert. I read in a Web site that when one rock band—which is sort of cooperative with the government in the sense that in every concert they sing a song that has religious overtones—was given a permit to have a concert, 20,000 young people bought tickets. They didn't have a venue large enough to accommodate everybody who wanted to attend. And whatever entertainment they do have is being curtailed by Ahmadinejad right now. So I think they are extremely persistent with the Internet because that's one way they've been able to overcome obstacles.

What's the rap scene like?

It's mostly youthful self-expression, and unlike some of its forms in the U.S., it's not misogynist. It's interesting, a few years ago, you would see slogans on buildings written by operatives of the regime saying that if you rap, you are a corrupt imitator of the West, or something like that. They tried to depict young people with any interest in western music, including rap, as traitors and good-for-nothings. Now even the *baseej* have a rap song (called "Amadeh Bash," or "We Are Prepared"), the lyrics of which, in effect, tell the United States that if they attack Iran, everyone is prepared to fight and resist them. The development and success of Persian rock music and rap have been instances where the government gave in to young people.

But it's being repressed now under Ahmadinejad?

They're beginning to. No permit has been granted for a rock concert in Tehran except for the one in mid-2006 that I just mentioned. Initially, Ahmadinejad did not want to portray himself as somebody who was going to clamp down on social freedoms. He played his cards well. He promised people a lot of economic benefits and more justice in the distribution of wealth. And then he began this whole nuclear discourse. In this case he rallied a lot of nationalist feeling around him. But there was a plan to curtail the social freedoms, to transform the whole structure of civil society as it had developed over the last decade. Therefore, we see the clampdowns on the bloggers, on the women's groups, on various reformists like [Ali-Akbar] Moussavi Khoini, who has been in prison since June 2006, and intellectuals like Ramin Jahanbegloo, who was released from prison in the fall of 2006.

The thing that interested me most was the crackdown on university professors. This was going on throughout the summer of 2006. They were forcing a lot of the secular and nonconservative Islamist university professors into retirement. And then in early fall, Ahmadinejad gave a speech, saying that for 150 years our entire educational system had been run by secular people who do not respect our traditions and our religion, and now we have to change that. In a sense he's advocating that students tell on their professors if they're not Islamist enough. It's a second cultural revolution, unfortunately, if they actually go through with it.

You spend time in Europe and speak French and Italian. How do the media in Europe report on Iran compared to the media in the United States?

There is more consistent and informed reporting on the entire Middle East, with more of a historical perspective. And there is more choice of different newspapers with a variety of perspectives available for the general reader. I find this is true in France, Italy, and in Britain, though in Britain some commercialization of the press has diminished the diversity of views, but it still exists. When something happens in the world, I find that when it is reported in the U.S. there is very little historical perspective. I don't mean that you have to report it with a fifty-page background to it. But someone who is writing or reporting an event who knows nothing or very little about the area sees it in a different way from someone who has read a few books and knows something about the history.

The Lebanon war is a case in point. It's depicted as Israel defending itself and trying to gain the release of its captured soldiers. If you look at it only within that context, you say, "They're right." But if you look at it in a slightly longer perspective than that day or that week, you see that these abductions have been going on *by both sides* for years in order to negotiate prisoner releases and, in fact, that the general picture is quite a bit more complicated than that little drawing that you get from the journalist who doesn't have the historical perspective.

I see this as the biggest problem with the American press. Its coverage of the Middle East is portrayed as "objective" and "fair" and "balanced," but in fact it is very biased and ideologically driven, and there isn't enough variety of perspectives. In Europe there are so many different political parties, as well as newspapers, with wide points of view that you have many interpretations and analyses of events, and you can make up your mind as an informed reader.

There has been a spate of books by Iranian-born writers writing in English, nonfiction as well as fiction. The most famous and popular has been Azar Nafisi's Reading Lolita in Tehran. *There is Marjane Satrapi's* Persepolis *and Azadeh Moaveni's* Lipstick Jihad. *What is your assessment of this literature?*

I think the more written about Iran from different points of view, the better. It's interesting that the genre that receives attention, like *Reading Lolita in Tehran*, *Lipstick Jihad*, and *Persepolis*, is the memoir. I've thought about it. How come the memoir? I've been involved in trying to get Iranian fiction, especially Iranian novels, published by mainstream publishers for years, and nobody wants to touch it. They say, "Who is going to read an Iranian novel?" or "Who cares? Foreign names, a different reality. Why should we publish it? It won't sell." But the memoir has been picked up by big publishing houses, and they have sold well. So I happen to think that if a good Iranian novel is picked up by a good publishing firm, it would sell, as well, as have translated novels from Latin America, from China, from all over the world.

Naguib Mahfouz of Egypt.

And Orhan Pamuk of Turkey. But the memoir in the Iranian context has a particular political component. First, because Iran has been so politicized, there is a stereotypical image of the country in the mind of most Americans. The ubiquitous television footage showing crowds chanting "Death to America," the black-turbaned, bearded clerics.

The poor political relations between the two countries, and its simplistic portrayal, have produced a uniform, one-dimensional view of that culture. So in a sense it's easier for the American public to digest the reality of one person at a time. Azar Nafisi wrote about her experience in the early years of the revolution through her own perspective. And I'm glad, actually, that that experience was balanced by books like *Persepolis* or even *Lipstick Jihad*.

But on another, more difficult political level, I think some works that can also be interpreted as Iran bashing, that can fit into the category of, "Oh, how liberating Nabokov or Austen is for them"— tend to gain more success. It's that kind of essentializing the Other that also has something to do with the success of some of these works. I'm referring to Nafisi's *Reading Lolita in Tehran.* I don't know whether she meant to portray it this way or not. She's a very smart, knowledgeable woman. And life was indeed difficult for women at that time in the many ways she eloquently describes. But the fact is that the publication of this book coincided with the time that Iran was designated as part of the "axis of evil." In that context, to read about what horrible things had been done in Iran to women assumed a different current meaning. It fit well with the axis-of-evil paradigm. And the interesting thing is that the book was referring to the years just after the revolution; it wasn't portraying the current situation of Iran. On the whole, it ended up affirming the stereotypes rather than challenging them, I think, and that was one of the reasons why it succeeded as much as it did in terms of sales and popularity.

The political use made of it after its publication is remarkable. Conservative think tanks discussed and promoted it vigorously. But I wouldn't put Satrapi's *Persepolis* in the same category. I think her book is a masterful portrayal of the incredible complexity of life after the revolution. Horror and humor are beautifully combined to convey the depth of the tragedies that occurred. And Moaveni's *Lipstick Jihad* is an interesting portrayal of how a person with two cultures, with dreams of returning home, can go there and actually live through the difficulties and become more mature in the love or critique of her two cultures. I found her book to be a captivating portrayal of the similarities and differences between the children of the revolution who grew up in Iran and those who grew up abroad.

On the whole, I think it's a good thing that a lot of books are being published on Iran. My reservation is that the choice of books that are presented to the general public isn't representative enough and is colored by commercial or political concerns.

Why has cinema developed so much in the post-Islamic-revolution period?

I think that it was one of the ways in which artists and filmmakers could express themselves creatively and get around the censor at the same time. They were very creative in doing this. I remember a discussion at an Iranian film festival that I attended at Lincoln Center. Someone brought up the fact that the stricter Islamist censorship had somehow challenged the artists to become more creative in the use of images and symbolism. They created new categories and a new visual language to bypass the censor. We had talented Iranian filmmakers even before the revolution, and we had very promising young students in film schools. The quality of the films produced after the revolution was due to the conjuncture of extremely good talent and an urge to be creative within great financial and political restraints. The third factor I would add is that we have a physically beautiful country; rich visual, written, and oral traditions; a terribly complex social and political culture—all good elements for the inspiration of artists.

There is an interesting discussion within Iran about the success of Iranian films abroad. Many people joke that Kiarostami or [Mohsen] Makhmalbaf, for example, make artsy films for foreign consumption. Many more films are made in Iran every year for the domestic market, and they draw large audiences within the country. Most of them deal with concrete problems of everyday people. Addiction, for example. We have one of the highest rates of heroin addiction among the youth now. A lot of the films are about women's issues.

Of those major names that are known in the West, we've discussed Kiarostami; you just mentioned Makhmalbaf. Other outstanding directors are Jafar Panahi and Majid Majidi. Are there any prominent women?

Rakhshan Bani-Etemad is the most accomplished. She makes documentaries as well as features, and her work has very strong social content, addressing poverty and women's issues. Then there is Pouran Derkhshandeh, who also works with documentary and features; Tahmineh Milani, who was actually arrested for making the film the *Hidden Half* (about left-wing students during the time of the shah who are suppressed at the time of the Islamic Republic); Samira Makhmalbaf, Mohsen Makhmalbaf's daughter (she made the film *The Apple* when she was seventeen); Maryam Shahriar; Marzieh Meshkini. All are extremely talented, brave women who address sensitive subjects, many having to do with the problems of women. I have to add that though he is a man, I consider Jafar Panahi to be one of the most feminist filmmakers we have. His films *The Circle* and most recently *Offside* were brilliant portrayals of the daily pressures on women and the complex and resilient ways they resist and prevail.

While we are on the subject of entertainment, I must mention the phenomenon of football, or soccer. It is possibly the activity that raises the most passion in Iran. There is an immense love of the game among men and women, young and old. It arouses national pride in the international sense, but soccer games are also used as a pretext for political expression and an arena for battling for women's rights. After the football riots of 2001, when people turned out in massive numbers to celebrate their team's victory and security forces attacked the crowds, the regime has retreated and allowed celebrations to go on. In June 2005, at the time of a very important game with Bahrain, one hundred women blocked the main entrance to Azadi Stadium in Tehran, protesting the law that does not allow women into stadiums. Some of them were let in after much pushing and shouting of slogans. But the law has not changed, and many women dress up as men to enter the stadium to see games. I would highly recommend the Jafar Panahi film *Offside*. It's about a few determined girls who dress up as boys to enter the stadium and how the different elements of the security forces deal with them. Whether motivated by political design or his own love of the game, even Ahmadinejad tried to waive the ban on women's presence in stadiums in April 2006, but he was overridden by the supreme leader and senior clerics, who said women should not see men in shorts running around, as it may arouse inappropriate sexual feelings. The members of the Campaign to Defend Women's Rights to Enter Sports Stadiums will not give up, however, and will persist to pressure the authorities in every peaceful way possible.

The fact remains that in today's Iran, everything can and almost does intersect with politics. The discourse of human rights and women's rights has entered and taken root in civil society and is here to stay, such that even monarchists and conservative Islamists have to address it in some way. This tough resolve by those who desire change within Iran, along with their equally strong determination to be independent of outside pressures and manipulations, should serve as a stern warning to the U.S. and other states who contemplate any military action against Iran.

Index

Index